BEAUTIFUL WEDDING DECORATIONS & GIFTS

ON A SMALL BUDGET

DIANE WARNER

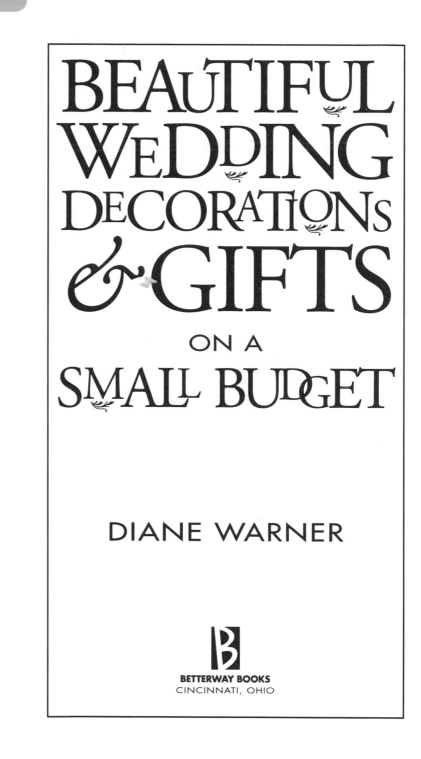

BETTERWAY BOOKS
CINCINNATI, OHIO

Acknowledgments

My biggest thanks go to my editor, David Tompkins, for his suggestions and encouragement. I would also like to thank my illustrator, Cathryn Cunningham, for her sweet, creative spirit. Cheryl Morrison, President of Abra Cadabra Gift Basket Magic, Inc., in Modesto, California, was an invaluable help to me, and I appreciate how she so generously revealed her one-of-a-kind trade secrets so I may share them with my readers.

I'm grateful to the staff at McHenry Museum who so lovingly explained wedding history and protocol. I am also grateful to all those clever, crafty women who shared their talents, and especially to one in particular—Lorraine Olson, whose joy and enthusiasm is contagious!

Library of Congress Cataloging-in-Publication Data

Warner, Diane
    Beautiful wedding decorations & gifts on a small budget / by Diane Warner.
        p.   cm.
    Includes index.
    ISBN 1-55870-393-4 (alk. paper)
    1. Handicraft. 2. Wedding decorations. 3. Weddings—Planning. I. Title
TT149.W28   1995
745.594'1—dc20   95-15217
                                                                               CIP

Edited by David Tompkins
Designed by Sandy Conopeotis Kent
Illustrations by Cathryn Cunningham

Table of Contents

DEDICATION

To Darren and Lisa

with love,

Mom

Introduction

*S*omeone you know getting married? Perhaps a daughter, son, sister or best friend? If so, I'm sure you're sharing the euphoric joy and anticipation of the upcoming wedding. Unfortunately, you may also be required to share your bank account! Whether you throw an engagement party, host the rehearsal dinner, plan the wedding and reception, or only need to bring a gift, you could use some creative, money-saving ideas.

I spent a year interviewing clever people who have learned some shortcuts: the tricks to theme decorating, the "creative assembly" of gift baskets, and the crafting of exquisite wedding accessories. This book contains *easy* projects for those of us who are short on time, talent or patience. Many of you are already juggling four jobs—career woman, homemaker, wife and mother. The last thing you need is some twelve-hour project that will only save you ten dollars!

This book is filled with over three hundred of the best ideas I could find; they are definitely the "biggest bangs for the buck"—easy, fast and affordable. Every one of you can tackle these projects with success.

A gift doesn't have to be expensive to look expensive; a party doesn't have to cost a mini-fortune to be a lot of fun; and you don't need to mortgage the homestead to afford a fairy-tale wedding!

1

Engagement Parties and Co-ed Showers

*N*ext to the wedding day itself, there's probably nothing quite as exciting as the day a couple becomes engaged, and it's perfectly understandable for them to drive up and down Main Street shouting to anyone who'll listen: "We're in love and we're getting married!" Then they race each other to the telephone to share their euphoric joy with every friend and relative they can think of. What they need to remember, however, is that, according to etiquette, both sets of parents should be told first, which is only logical. After all, wouldn't it be embarrassing if the bride's mother heard about the engagement from her hairdresser?

Once the parents have been told, however, the couple is free to send out a news release over the Associated Press if they'd like. The next step is for the parents to meet each other, followed by a formal or informal engagement party where the couple is toasted and congratulated and the bride's and groom's families can get to know each other. The bride's parents usually host this celebration; however, depending on the circumstances, it can also be hosted by the groom's parents or any other relatives of the bride or groom. The party may be casual or formal, and there may or may not be gifts.

Another type of party that has become quite popular is the co-ed shower; this may be hosted by anyone and always includes gifts for the couple.

Whether the celebration is an engagement party or co-ed shower, it may be formal or casual, held indoors or out, at a restaurant or around a backyard swimming pool. If the party is to be formal, you will want to send engraved or printed invitations. If informal, you may send simple handwritten notes or invite guests over the telephone.

FORMAL INVITATIONS

There are several ways you can create elegant, yet affordable, invitations. One way is to originate them on a computer, printing onto high-quality 6″ × 9″ bordered stationery using a laser or ink-jet printer. If you don't have access to a computer, have a "master" made up by a calligrapher; this "master" can then be copied at a quick-print shop.

Here is sample wording for a formal invitation:

YOU ARE INVITED TO AN

ENGAGEMENT LUNCHEON

IN HONOR OF

JASON AND MELODY

ON SATURDAY, NOVEMBER 27,

ONE IN THE AFTERNOON,

AT THE CLUBHOUSE

AT BEL AIR PLACE,

2200 NORTH BRIARWOOD,

HOSTED BY THE

BRIDE'S PARENTS,

JIM AND TRUDY BANKS.

RSVP (210) 663-9990

INFORMAL INVITATIONS

An informal invitation may be as simple as this handwritten note:

Dear Bill and Cindy,
Did you hear about Jason and Melody? They're getting married on New Year's Day and we're throwing them a couple's shower this Saturday night at our house. We're cooking up hot dogs and hamburgers on the grill, so dress casual. Give us a call if you can come.
Thanks,
Jim and Trudy
663-9990

Party Theme Decorations

Traditionally, engagement parties are more formal than showers, but in this day and age anything goes. Here are a few formal and informal party ideas:

SIT-DOWN DINNER

You can make this type of party as fancy and formal as you like, depending on the setting. If you have several tables, which you probably will if you invite a large group of family and friends, you'll need to decorate each one. Start with white linen or lace tablecloths and fancy-folded linen napkins, plus a floral or candle centerpiece for each table (see chapter three.) Then add the finest crystal, silver and china place settings you can find. (Borrow from Mom or Grandma for the occasion.)

SPRING GARDEN PARTY

If you take the party outside you'll have the advantage of a naturally romantic setting. Set up individual tables, each with its own tablecloth and napkins, centerpiece and place cards, but instead of fine china and crystal, you may use your less expensive pottery dishes and glassware, or even paper plates. By the way, anytime you use paper plates when entertaining, splurge and buy the best. Following the outdoor garden party theme, use ordinary clay flowerpots as centerpieces, each filled with a different plant, such as azaleas, petunias or geraniums. Buy the flowers in the same colors—all white or pink, for example—then wrap a color-coordinated ribbon around the top of each pot. An economical substitute for ribbon is gingham fabric cut in strips with pinking shears (watch for sales at your fabric store). If the party is in the evening, you may want to add votive candles at each table and string patio lights. Plain or helium-filled balloons, along with crepe paper streamers, will add a festive look to the garden.

WINE AND CHEESE TASTING PARTY

This is a good choice for an engagement party because it's easy to plan and host. If several family members are hosting the party together, have them bring various wines, cheeses and crackers. Set up a table with tablecloth, napkins and a centerpiece; add fine china and crystal wine glasses or paper plates and plastic wine glasses. Again, balloons will spread a little color.

COUNTRY-WESTERN BACKYARD BARBECUE

Here's an informal, fun party idea where you can carry the theme to the hilt: Ask the guests to wear western outfits; decorate with lariats, cowboy hats, saddles, branding irons, single-trees, red bandanas, potted cactus plants or bales of hay. If your guests are into country-western line dancing, rent a dance floor and hire a western band or play taped music. A red checkered tablecloth is perfect, along with a rustic sign that says: "Bob and Anna are Gettin' Hitched" or "Bob and Anna—Ridin' Off into the Sunset Together!" By the way, real cowboys don't cotton to balloons, so you can forget them for this party.

NOSTALGIA PARTY

Here's one of the best ideas yet—a chance to secretly collect memorabilia from the couple's past to use as decorations: baby pictures, awards, Little League uniforms, cheerleading pom-poms, old high school or college yearbooks, etc. Dress up two teddy bears as "bride" and "groom" (preferably the bride's and groom's own childhood bears, if they exist). You will need to make a veil for the teddy bear bride and a top hat for the groom. The veil is easily created by gathering a piece of white lace or tulle netting and attaching to the top of the "bride's" head (between her ears) with a white silk flower. The top hat can be made out of black construction paper (see the pattern below). If you really want to go all out, you can fashion a wedding gown and tux, but the veil and top hat are plenty. Try to drape the "groom's" arm over the "bride's" shoulder.

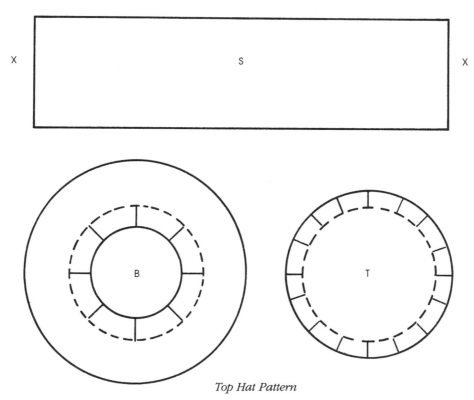

Top Hat Pattern

Enlarge this pattern so that piece *S* (the side of the hat) is ½ inch longer than needed to wrap around the head of your teddy bear.

Directions for top hat

- *Piece* S *(side of hat)* Overlap the ends (Xs) by ½ inch; tape or glue to hold.
- *Piece* B *(brim of hat)*: Cut out the center; fold at dotted lines, snipping where indicated to create flaps that will tuck up into the bottom of piece S; glue or tape these flaps for a tight fit.
- *Piece* T *(top of hat)*: Fold at the dotted lines and snip where indicated, creating flaps; tuck these flaps inside the top of piece S and glue or tape to hold in place.

POLYNESIAN POOL PARTY

Everyone loves this type of "hang-loose," relaxed, happy party. Ask the guests to dress "Hawaiian." Fashion flower leis for the engaged couple using silk flowers or fresh blooms from your garden. (By the way, this is a good time to mention that any time I suggest using silk flowers, always tear the blossoms from the stems and glue them back tightly before arranging the flowers. Otherwise, they may come apart.) Add Tiki torches, rafts of fresh flowers floating in the pool, Hawaiian music, and a buffet table full of typical Polynesian fare: roast pork, fresh pineapple, bowls of fresh coconut, grilled fish, melons, strawberries, salads, loaves of sweet Hawaiian bread, sweet potatoes and, of course, a bowl of poi. (Guests love to taste the stuff so they can complain that "it tastes like wallpaper paste." I always wonder how people *know* this; I don't remember eating wallpaper paste in my whole life!)

A POUNDIN'

The idea of this party is that, in addition to the traditional gift, each guest also brings "a pound of something" for the bride or groom. The bride might receive a pound of flour, sugar, coffee, bubble bath crystals, potpourri, etc. The groom may receive a pound of nails, golf tees, pipe tobacco, pretzels, mixed nuts or jelly beans. Let the couple's hobbies trigger ideas for this "a poundin' party." Use an old-fashioned balance scale as the foundation for your floral centerpiece.

OTHER PARTY THEMES

- Happy New Year
- Be My Valentine
- Costume Party
- Progressive Dinner
- Seasonal (Christmas wedding? Harvest wedding?)
- Beach Party
- Fifties Sock Hop
- Ethnic (Scandinavian, Mexican, German, Oriental, etc.)

Gifts

As I already mentioned, an engagement party may or may not include gifts for the couple, but a shower always does. Here are some gift suggestions that are especially suitable for either of these parties:

Basket Gifts

The trendy fad of the nineties is to give gift baskets, no matter what the occasion. The most mediocre gift looks dramatically exciting (and expensive) when it's nested in a basket. By the time you add a little filler, such as wood shavings or a colorful napkin, plus a silk flower or two, some ribbon, and a couple of novelty items, your ordinary gift will seem like "more." If you don't know what I mean, just wander into a gift shop and examine the forty-dollar and fifty-dollar gift baskets; you'll find that the high prices result from the artistic, creative assembly of several items that, if purchased separately on the discount market, may cost less than fifteen dollars total.

Here are ten gift basket ideas that are clever and unique. By the way, every one of these gift baskets can be expanded with more ingredients in case several guests want to go together on the cost.

HONEYMOON PICNIC BASKET

Material

- A deep wicker basket or an actual picnic basket with hinged lid
- 1 yard of red and white checked napkin fabric
- Red plastic cutlery and plates, plus clear plastic champagne glasses and checkered paper napkins
- Woven wicker paper plate holders
- Raffia or red gingham ribbon
- Strawflower or a silk flower
- A bottle of wine or sparkling cider
- Plastic sack of homemade caramel corn
- Plastic sack of homemade cookies
- Gourmet picnic items of your choice, such as:
  - Bagel chips
  - Biscuits
  - Beef stick or German beer sausage
  - Sweet-hot or Dijon mustard

Pickled asparagus
Any cheeses
Fudge or any candies

Directions

The first three items are the basics; the rest is up to you. Shop carefully, looking for bargains at your discount outlets and import shops. Your best source of baskets is garage sales, even if you need to spray paint those baskets back to life.

Once you've assembled everything you need, place the items in the basket in such a way that they seem to be "bulging" over the top. Decorate the handle of the basket with a raffia bow and strawflower or a red gingham ribbon and silk flower. (See the opening page of this chapter.)

HONEYMOON BEACH BASKET
Materials

The same materials listed for the Honeymoon Picnic Basket with any of these added items:

- Suntan lotion
- Small shovel and pail (filled with hard candies)
- Two beach "pillows"
- Frisbie
- Sunglasses
- Beach towels

This basket can become a little pricey unless you go together with several other people or find good buys on some of the items, such as the sunglasses and beach towels. The beach "pillow," by the way, is a clever addition you can make yourself out of a yard of plastic fabric. Just fold it in half, sew the sides together and close the top with Velcro. Then when the couple is at the beach all they have to do is fill these covers with sand and they will have instant pillows; these clever pillows can be emptied and folded back into the basket when they leave the beach. You can make inexpensive beach towels, too, by purchasing two 3-yard lengths of terry cloth that you finish on each end with bias tape or by turning under and stitching on your sewing machine or by hand.

LIVE OR SILK PLANT IN A BASKET

This is a simple idea that makes for a very attractive party gift. Take any live or silk plant you find on sale and nestle it down into a basket filled with excelsior or tissue paper. Add a large raffia or crinkle ribbon and you will have a gift that definitely looks more expensive than the few dollars you have invested. If the plant is one especially selected for the yard or window box of the couple's new home or apartment, you might want to add a garden trowel or a pair of colorful garden gloves.

BASKET OF GARDENING SUPPLIES

If the engaged couple loves to garden and you know this for a fact, what could be more appropriate than a basket filled with gardening supplies?

Walk into any discount nursery and let your imagination run wild. In addition to the trowel and garden gloves mentioned above, how about seeds, fertilizer spikes, snail bait, rose spray, potting soils or small garden tools, such as pruning shears?

LOVE BASKET

Line a basket with a homemade "bear rug," then fill with massage lotions, bubble bath, scented candles, chocolates and a CD or cassette tape of the couple's favorite romantic music. Make the "bear rug" out of ordinary velour or synthetic fake fur fabric. Use the pattern shown opposite to cut a "bear skin" out of the fabric; then hem it by hand or on your sewing machine. Enlarge the pattern to any size. A small "bear rug," about the size of a large table napkin, will be a cute novelty basket liner, or you can make one big enough to actually roll around on in front of the fireplace!

GOURMET COFFEE BASKET

This is a perfect idea for the couple who is really into gourmet coffees. Shop for a variety of coffee beans on sale (less expensive if purchased in bulk); bag them up in small plastic bags with clever computer-generated, calligraphied or hand-drawn labels. Line the basket with a colorful napkin or placemat. If you feel like splurging a little or know of another guest who may want to go in on this gift, add an electric coffee grinder and a couple of coffee mugs. A coffee grinder usually costs about twenty dollars in a retail store, but sometimes you see them at discount stores for under fifteen dollars.

SOUP BASKET

Fill a napkin-lined basket with several packages of soup mixes, such as Mrs. Grass' Onion or Homestyle Vegetable or Campbell's Oriental Ramen Noodle Soup Mix; add a couple of crockery soup mugs. A clever trick is to purchase plastic packages of uncooked beans or split-peas right off your grocery store shelf, open them and re-package into your own clear plastic bags. Label each bag and tie with raffia bows. Top them off with your own "home-made" soup recipes which you have surreptitiously copied right off the store packages onto attractive cards, also tied at the neck of each bag. One of the most colorful and interesting ideas to use for this deliciously deceptive plan is a package of "fifteen bean soup" purchased for pennies straight from your grocer's shelf.

Bear Rug Pattern

"FIRST HOME" BASKET

This is a gift basket suitable for any engaged couple because, unless they're moving in with relatives (heaven forbid!), they will be living in their own home or apartment and they'll need one of these practical gifts, also known as a "junk drawer basket." Picture your own junk drawer at home and go out and purchase the same kinds of stuff: small hammer, regular and Phillips screwdrivers, matches, refrigerator magnets, extension cord, a pair of pliers, a tube of household cement, tacks, nails, screws, bolts, hooks, cellophane tape, scissors, measuring tape, masking tape, hole punch, stapler, note paper, flashlight, extra batteries, etc. This gift will become a real conversation piece as each guest recalls the weird things stored in his own "junk drawer."

HONEYMOON TRAVEL BASKET

This can be a really creative gift, especially if you know the couple's peculiarities or their honeymoon destination. Fill the basket with maps or guidebooks for their honeymoon location, along with an address book, stationery, stamps, pens, travel iron, sewing kit, first-aid kit, sunscreen, insect repellant, Lysol room spray, snacks to eat on the airplane, candy, film, matching sun visors or fannie-packs, plus items related to the things they plan to do, such as golf balls or tees, tennis balls or sweat bands, underwater goggles, etc. You can personalize the sun visors or fannie-packs with their names by using a liquid embroidery pen. These are available at any craft store.

FIRST CHRISTMAS BASKET

This is a gift that's appropriate regardless of when the couple plans to be married, because there *will* be a Christmas coming up within their first year of marriage. This basket is easy to put together because we all know what they'll need: tree decorations, including lights and ornaments, silk mistletoe balls, Christmas candles, napkins, paper plates, gift wrap, tape, gift tags, and a small pair of scissors. You may want to purchase a "First Christmas" ornament or customize one yourself with the couple's names and wedding date. (There are directions in chapter five.) As a special touch, why not add a homemade string of popcorn? Use a 9-foot length of white dental floss and a huge craft needle to string the popcorn. If several of you want to go together on this gift, you may want to splurge and purchase a collector item, such as a manger scene or an angel or star for the top of the tree.

Other Gift Ideas

CELEBRATION CRATE

Here's another conversation piece for the party: an ordinary wooden crate lined with wood shavings or tissue paper, then filled with as many bottles of wine or champagne as you wish, depending on how many people are going in on this gift. Each bottle is to be opened on a special day during the couple's first year of marriage: their first New Year's Eve, Valentine's Day, Christmas, wedding anniversary and birthdays. You can even add one for their "Kiss-and-Make-Up-After-Our-First-Fight" celebration. You can go crazy with this crate by embellishing each bottle with novelties, such as party hats and horns, streamers, packaged banners that say "Happy Birthday," or a sprig of artificial mistletoe tied to the neck of their Christmas bottle. You can also add "extras," such as a corkscrew or snacks for each occasion. You can even tuck in little wrapped gifts with tags that say things like "Don't open until Anna's birthday." It can be a lot of fun for several people to go together on this celebration crate, but it also works well with only two or three bottles tied at their necks with tags: "Our First Christmas," "Our First New Year's Eve," or "Our First Anniversary." (See the opening page of this chapter.)

ANNIVERSARY VASE

Although this is a very inexpensive gift to assemble, it won't look it by the time you get it together. You will need a vase, preferably tall and white, plus a dozen long-stemmed red silk roses. The idea of this gift is for the couple to reaffirm their vows on each wedding anniversary, as they place one of the roses into the vase. So, on their first anniversary, the vase will contain one rose, and by their twelfth, there will, of course, be twelve roses. The vase can be embellished with ribbon if you like, but you will need to add a note to the roses that says:

> "Add one rose to this vase as you reaffirm your vows on each wedding anniversary."

For a dramatic effect, try to find a long white flower gift box, even if you have to purchase one from a florist.

"OUR FIRST CHRISTMAS" YULE LOG

Take a plain fireplace log approximately 2 feet long. Cover it with fake or live evergreen sprays (use live greens if the wedding is close to Christmas), then add dried apple slices, dried white gypsophila, and a large red paper twist ribbon in the center. Be sure to add a tag that says, "Bob and Anna's First Christmas," or "Our First Yule Log," etc. The twist ribbon and dried gypsophila are available at your local craft and floral supply store. I'll tell you a secret: They won't have the heart to burn it, first yule log or not, because it will be so darned cute!

"DO NOT DISTURB" SIGN

This gift will stir up some interesting comments. Use the pattern on page 15 to make a heart-shaped, lacy, embroidered "Do Not Disturb" sign to hang on their honeymoon hotel doorknob. (Enlarge the pattern until the heart is about 9 inches wide.) Cut two of the "hearts"

Yule Log

out of any white satiny fabric; embroider or use a liquid embroidery pen to write "Do Not Disturb" on the right side of one of the hearts. Place the right sides together and sew by hand or on your sewing machine, leaving a 3-inch opening at the bottom. Turn the heart right-side-out and fill with polyester fill, cotton batting, or shreds of tissue or paper towel. Close the 3-inch opening with small stitches, using your machine or sewing by hand. Use craft glue or a hot glue gun to attach ruffled lace around the outside of the heart, saving one length of lace to use as a hanger at the top of the heart.

WEDDING VIDEO BOX

Spray the front, spine and back of a plastic videotape box with spray adhesive glue, then wrap with white satin acetate fabric, tucking all the edges under as you go. By cutting the fabric 11 inches wide by 9 inches high, you will have at least ½ inch extra for this purpose. Use clothespins to hold the edges down until the glue is completely dry. Use the same glue or a hot glue gun to attach ruffled eyelet lace around the edges of the videotape box; then embellish with dainty accessories, such as narrow white satin ribbons, streamers of tiny white pearls, small silk flowers or wedding appliques, such as love doves or wedding bells. Use your imagination and you'll end up with a very special, yet inexpensive, gift.

WEDDING MEMORABILIA BOX

A wedding memorabilia box is used to save all those bulky items that won't lie flat in a scrapbook or photo album, such as the groom's pressed boutonniere, their champagne toasting glasses, the ring bearer's pillow or, perhaps, the bride's preserved bouquet. Find a sturdy box that has a separate lid, even a shoe box will do, especially a golf shoe box or boot box. The lid needs to have a "padded top," so the first step is to glue down a piece of quilt batting cut to the exact size of the top of the lid. Cover the lid with taffeta or cotton moire fabric, using spray adhesive glue, folding under the raw edges. Next, cover the inside of the lid, plus the inside and outside of the box itself with any white satiny fabric, also

*Heart
Pattern*

folding under the raw edges as you go. Once the box and lid are securely covered, you are ready to "decorate." Use a hot glue gun or tube of fabric glue to mount your decorations. Here are some common notions used to embellish a memorabilia box:

- Satin ribbons or bows
- Silk flowers
- Appliques
- A small, framed photo of the couple
- Small, framed baby pictures of the couple
- Flat or ruffled lace
- Braiding
- Pearl beads or pearl streamers
- Tassles
- Silk ivy leaves
- Tiny lace bells or white doves, according to the theme of the wedding
- Embroidery thread or liquid embroidery pens to "write" a saying on top of the lid, such as *Our Beautiful Beginning* or *Our Wedding Treasures*

Just as with the wedding video box, there is no "right" or "wrong," and you will have a lot of fun making a gift that will be cherished for years to come.

WEDDING SCRAPBOOK

Purchase a large scrapbook that has plenty of pages; ignore the cover design because you're going to cover it anyway. Use the same instructions given above for the Wedding Memorabilia Box. On the first page of the scrapbook you can mount the wedding invitation or simply write in the couple's names and wedding date.

BRIDE AND GROOM TOASTING GLASSES

Take two plain, fluted champagne glasses and decorate them to be used by the bride and groom at their wedding reception. A good place to shop for these glasses is at a factory outlet shopping center where you may find quality crystal for only two dollars each. Tie satin ribbon and tiny, silk flowers to the stems of the glasses, or perhaps miniature doves or bells, according to the wedding's theme.

NAMEPLATE FOR THE COUPLE'S HOME

Whether your talent is ceramics, woodworking, leather working or tole painting, you can make a nameplate for the couple's front door, porch rail or lamppost. If you like to work with wood or leather, you can burn in the names on a rectangular piece, adding a strap or hook for hanging. If your craft is ceramics, you can form, bake and paint a heart-shaped sign, leaving a hole for hanging. Tole painting (a type of folk art, using acrylic paint and a variety of brush strokes) is a practical way to convert old things (shovels, wagon wheels, weathered wood, milk cans, etc.) into treasured gifts. Take an old milk can, for example; spray paint it blue; then tole paint daisies around the couple's names, such as "The Bryans" or "Bob and Anna Cooper."

KEEPSAKE WEDDING PILLOW

If you like to embroider or cross-stitch, this is the perfect gift for you to make. Enlarge the heart-shaped pattern shown earlier in this chapter to cut two pieces from satin acetate fabric, embroidering the couple's names and wedding date on the front of one of the pieces. Sew the two pieces together (right sides facing each other), leaving a 3-inch opening at the bottom of the heart. Turn the heart right-side-out and fill with polyester fill, closing the 3-inch opening with small hemming stitches. Use a hot glue gun or hand stitches to attach 2-inch-wide ruffled lace around the edges of the heart. Add pearl streamers, narrow satin ribbon and tiny silk flowers in the upper left corner of the heart, above the couple's names.

FRAMED WEDDING INVITATION

Take the wedding invitation you have received in the mail and place it in an attractive frame, complete with matting if you like, and you'll have an affordable, yet appropriate, engagement party gift. Every couple appreciates a framed copy of their wedding invitation to display in their home.

*Wedding Pillow and
Framed Invitation*

HONEYMOON MEMORY BOOK

Purchase a "wordless book" at your local stationery store or book store, plus one yard of a coordinating grosgrain or satin ribbon from a fabric store. Using a calligraphy pen, fill in the first page of the book with the couple's names, wedding date and honeymoon destination. Then glue the center point of the ribbon to the middle of the book's spine; wrap the ribbon around the book, tying in a bow where the pages meet. Cut off any excess ribbon. This gift is to be used by the couple to record honeymoon memories of endearments spoken, special feelings, love notes, poems, or impressions of their honeymoon destination.

FAMILY HEIRLOOMS

It is appropriate and appreciated for a family member to give an heirloom to a newly engaged couple. Perhaps you have an antique lace tablecloth, tea kettle or hand-carved picture frame that has been handed down through the years. When you give one of these treasures as a gift, it not only conveys love and thoughtfulness, but a real warm welcome to the man or woman who will soon become part of your family. Warning: This type of sentimental gift often brings tears!

FRAMED PHOTO OF THE COUPLE

Newly engaged couples *love* to see photos of themselves together! You see, it is still a novelty to them that they are soon to be a permanent twosome and they are a bit in awe of the idea. So, even if you only have a good snapshot of the couple, have it enlarged, then place it in a white or brass oval frame.

GIFT OF YOUR TALENTS

Now, here's an economical idea! Use your computer or calligraphy pen to compose a gift certificate good for something you will do for the couple after they're married. You might offer to wallpaper a room in their new home, or bring them a dozen cookies every month for a year, or cook and deliver a hot dinner any night of their choice, or perhaps there is a child involved from a previous marriage and you can offer "One Night of Babysitting—Your Home or Mine." Believe me, this type of creative gift will be appreciated much more than any ten fake silver trays!

GRAPEVINE DOOR WREATH

Whether the couple will be living in a home, condo or apartment, they *will* have a front door, so this gift is sure to be appreciated. Purchase a circular or heart-shaped grapevine wreath, approximately 15 inches high. You'll also need some florist's tape, a hot glue gun, waxed artificial ivy, and silk flowers of your choice (roses, daisies, mums and peonies work well). Using the florist's tape, attach the ivy to the circumference of the wreath, then add the flowers and attach a wire at the top of the wreath for hanging. A clever "newlywed" idea is to make a "cupid's wreath" by using the grapevine woven into a heart shape and "shooting" an arrow through it diagonally. Just cut a 30-inch length of any straight branch (a willow branch works well). Add a sprig of ivy at the lower end of the arrow and a couple of silk flowers at the "arrow end." This is a charmingly romantic gift for the engaged couple, and with very little expense.

Wreath and Decorated Bottle

DRESSED-UP CHAMPAGNE BOTTLE

Here is a way to convert an ordinary bottle of champagne into a special gift. Cover the bottle with the sleeve and cuff of a man's long-sleeved white dress shirt. Simply cut off the sleeve, then slip the bottle into the sleeve with the neck sticking out the top of the cuff. The cuff now becomes the bottle's "collar." Allow enough fabric to fold under the bottle and glue to the bottom with a hot glue gun. Tie a black "bow tie" (made from grosgrain or satin ribbon) around the "collar" at the neck of the bottle, and you'll have a unique engagement gift.

"His" and "Hers" Gifts

These are perfect for engagement parties or co-ed showers, because they're not only a lot of fun, but they give both the bride and groom a gift to open. Embroider the individual names on these gifts, using regular embroidery thread or a liquid embroidery pen.

"HIS" AND "HERS" PAJAMAS

He gets the "bottoms" and she gets the "top" of a pair of men's pajamas. This will get some laughs.

"HIS" AND "HERS" APRONS

Purchase inexpensive "generic" aprons and personalize them with the couple's names, or make the aprons yourself out of heavy cotton or denim fabric (1¼ yards for each apron). You can use the pattern shown on page 20 by enlarging it so that each apron is about 27 inches long (from neck to bottom hem) and 36 inches wide around the bottom of the apron. Cut four pieces of grosgrain ribbon, 1-inch-wide belting or cotton cording, each about 25 inches long, which will be used as ties for the back and neck of each apron. Turn under and stitch down every raw edge of the apron and attach the four ties at the letters *N* and *T*.

"HIS" AND "HERS" DAYPACKS

Find two bright daypacks on sale; then customize them with the couple's names using a waterproof liquid embroidery pen in case they get caught in the rain.

"HIS" AND "HERS" PILLOWCASES

Shop around for a white sale and pick up a quality pair of pillowcases. What will make them special, of course, is their names embroidered on each one.

Magical, Affordable Gift Wrap

As we all know, it's easy to spend more on gift wrap than the gift itself! It can be disheartening, in fact, to "shop 'til you drop" looking for a bargain, only to blow all the money you've saved on gift wrap. Wouldn't you like to give your gifts the "Tiffany look" for only pennies? Well, I've talked to a lot of clever people, and here's how they do it:

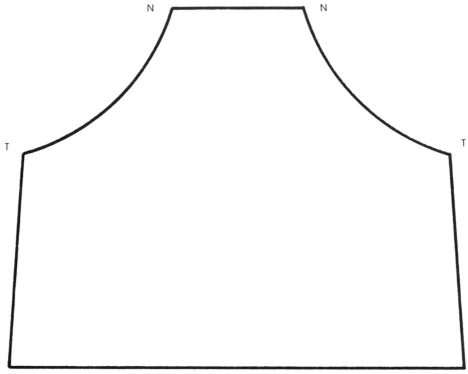

Apron Pattern

GIFT BAGS

We all know that the use of gift bags is easy, fast and foolproof, even for the klutziest among us! These bags don't come cheap, however, so we need to learn how to make them ourselves.

1 Use bags you already have around the house, from brown or colored lunch bags to those bags with plastic handles from specialty shops, cosmetics counters, etc. The lunch bags have no logos, of course, but the store bags usually do, so you merely glue something decorative on top of the logo—and presto!—you have an original gift bag. Start collecting these bags, along with the fronts of greeting cards, pieces of fabric, patterned paper or decorative artwork that can be cut to cover the logos. Then, add touches of ribbon, silk or fresh flowers or greenery, along with any novelty notions that fit the occasion, including stickers that can be purchased by the sheet at your local grocery store.

2 Make a large or small tote bag, using the pattern opposite (enlarge it to the size you want). A small gift bag is usually about 9 inches high by 7 inches wide; a large one is about 16 inches high by 20 inches wide.

Once you've enlarged your pattern, cut two pieces from any heavy cotton or synthetic fabric; place the pieces with right sides together and stitch on the dotted lines. Then pull the bag "open" and stitch the bottom at the dotted lines (see opposite). Turn inside and stitch down the top edge of the bag. Buy a package of colored shoelaces (about 22 inches long)

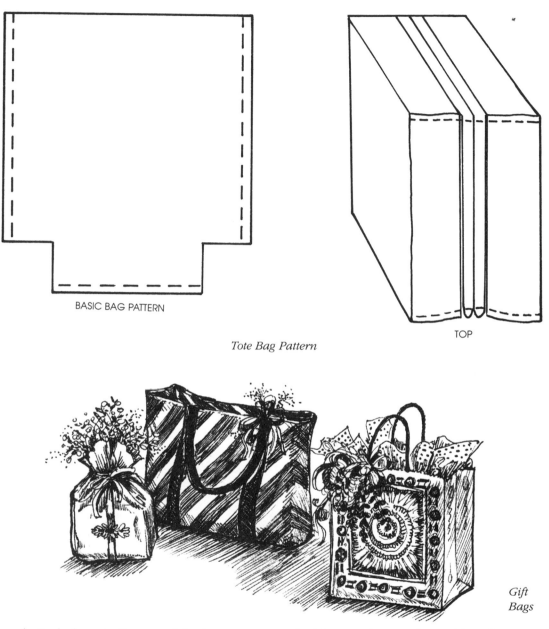

BASIC BAG PATTERN

Tote Bag Pattern

TOP

Gift Bags

and attach them to the top of the bag, one on each side, creating two looped handles. Line the bag with tissue paper. *Optional*: Cut a piece of colored cardboard to fit the bottom of the bag.

GIFT BOXES

Enlarge the pattern on page 22 to any size you need; trace it onto stiff paper or light cardboard. Cut on all the solid lines and fold on the dotted lines. Glue the top flap (*X*) to the

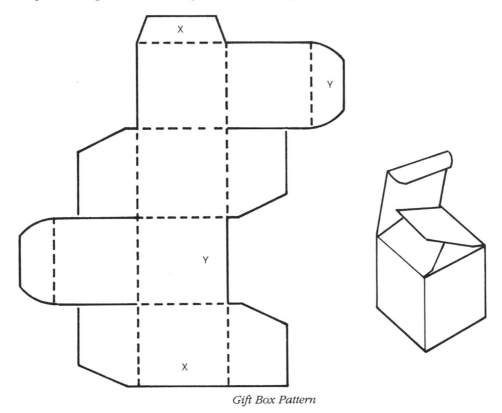

Gift Box Pattern

inside of the lower *X.* Then glue the side flap (*Y*) to the inside of the lower *Y.* Make the box out of decorative paper or poster board and you won't even need to wrap it; you'll only need a bow. See if you can find stiff paper or poster board that is shiny gold or silver; topped off with a gold or silver ribbon, your gift will have a very professional look.

CREATIVE GIFT WRAP

Here are practical alternatives to expensive gift wrapping paper:

- Shelving paper.
- Wallpaper.
- A plastic tablecloth.
- Newspapers: Use the *Wall Street Journal* or sports sections to wrap men's gifts, the fashion pages for women's gifts. (Iron the sheets first to give them body and take out the creases.)
- Colored tissue paper (bought in bulk).
- New or used fabrics: Use pinking shears to cut the fabric to the right size for your gift. Watch for "glamorous" dresses or skirts at garage sales; any shiny, lacy, sparkly fabric will work. Also, shop the "remnant bins" at your local fabric shop. These fabrics can also be cut into strips that can be used to tie the gifts after they're wrapped.

- Sponge-painted paper: Use an irregularly shaped, porous sponge to dab poster paint onto plain white or brown butcher paper.
- Iron-on-crayon paper: Place crayon shavings over butcher paper and cover with waxed paper. Iron on top of the waxed paper.
- Maps, posters: These make interesting gift wraps.
- Dinner-sized napkins: Use flowered, checkered or children's party napkins to wrap small- to medium-sized gifts.
- Bottles, jars, tins, cardboard tubes, Chinese-food cartons, baskets, toy buckets, coffee mugs, etc. Start collecting unusual containers for your gifts; you'll find a half dozen at every garage sale, and priced at only twenty-five cents each! All you need is a little imagination. Can't you picture that old Mason jar, filled with homemade biscotti, wrapped in cellophane and tied at the neck with a couple of cinnamon sticks and a gingham bow?

TIFFANY TOPPERS

Now we come to the best part of all—those cute and clever adornments that dress up your package. When you have a gift professionally wrapped in a department store, have you noticed those extra toppers they place on your gift package? They make the gift special, and you can do the same. Use doilies or pieces of lace, stickers, fresh or silk flowers, evergreens from your garden, pine cones, a strand of pearls, or a stick of candy. If it's a gift for a bride's kitchen shower, tie in a spatula or wooden spoon. See how easy it is? Start training your eye to little treasures that can be added to a gift. You'll find a lot of these gems at garage sales. For example, remember the inevitable box of junk jewelry? You may find a strand of beads or pearls that can be worked around a bow or flower. It gives another grand purpose to scouting garage sales!

2

Bridal Showers

*A*n addition to any engagement parties or co-ed showers, the bride is usually "showered" again with gifts at a party planned especially for her. This idea grew from the age-old tradition of the dowry, which is money, property or household goods brought to the marriage by the bride. The story is told of the poor miller who had generously given all his goods to the poor and had nothing left for his daughter's dowry. The townspeople felt sorry for the family and "showered" the bride with enough money and goods that she could marry without shame.

A bridal shower is usually hosted by the maid or matron of honor or by the bridesmaids. It may also be hosted by a relative, friend or co-worker. The party may be formal or informal, polite and proper, or fun and silly.

Party Theme Decorations

You'll want your party theme to be special and memorable, a departure from the "same old thing." Let your imagination run wild; here are a few ideas to start your creative juices flowing:

KITCHEN SHOWER

The gifts for a kitchen shower range from small appliances to cookie sheets to spice racks to mixing bowls. Here are some decorating ideas:

Kitchen Grater Luminaries

Wrap a dinner sized plate in foil; place a white votive candle in the center of the plate; cover the candle with an ordinary, metal kitchen grater; place fresh flowers and greenery around the grater, filling the outer edge of the plate. The candlelight will flicker through the openings in the grater. Use several in the room, on the serving table, or as centerpieces on individual tables.

Decorated Recipe Box

Turn a plain 4″ × 6″ index box into a party decoration by hot-glueing tiny silk stephanotis, wedding bells, love doves, seed pearls, sequins, lace or ribbon onto the sides and lid of the box. Send each guest four index cards they are to bring to the shower, complete with their favorite recipes. This recipe box will then, of course, become a joint shower gift.

Towel and Dishrag Place Settings

Use kitchen towels as place mats and colorful dishrags as napkins.

HEIRLOOM SHOWER

This is a wonderful party theme for a family shower. Each relative (or future relative) brings a family heirloom as a shower gift. Here are some decorating ideas:

Wedding Gown Display

Have your guests dig out their wedding gowns to put on display as the center of your party decor. You can use mannequins or dress forms to "model" the dresses, or you can hang several gowns on white satin covered hangers to display around the room. A fashion show may be in order if any of the dresses can still be worn. If a woman has "outgrown" her wedding gown, she may ask her daughter or niece to model it at the party.

Photo Display

Cover a table with a white lace tablecloth and display as many family wedding photos as you can find. Your guests will spend a lot of time around this table recalling the silly things that went wrong at some of the weddings or comparing the various wedding gowns. When the bride-to-be opens her heirloom gifts, by the way, these photos will come in handy to identify the original owners of these family treasures.

CHRISTMAS ORNAMENT SHOWER

The idea of this shower, of course, is to furnish the new bride with ornaments for her first Christmas tree. By spreading your own Christmas decorations over the room and onto the serving table, you will have a colorful, yet affordable, shower.

Christmas Tree

Use a tree as the focal point for your theme. It may be your own artificial tree that you assemble for the party, or a live, potted or synthetic tree given to the bride as a hostess gift. Each guest brings an ornament or other tree decoration as a shower gift; hang the ornaments on the tree as they are opened. Give the tree a little "help" by tying it with ribbons (in the wedding colors) and wrapping it with a long garland of popcorn you have strung in advance.

VICTORIAN TEA PARTY

This type of elegant party is illustrated on the opening page of this chapter.

The Table With the Victorian Touch

The focal point of this shower is the serving table itself. Scatter it with as many delicate, Victorian-style decorations as you can find: a pair of lacy gloves, a tiny silk tussie mussie, heart-shaped boxes, potpourri bags, photos of Grandma and Grandpa on their wedding day; a hand-painted tea set, antique cups and saucers, old-fashioned tongs and tea balls.

A GIFT BASKET SHOWER

Every guest brings a gift basket for the bride-to-be, such as a Tea-Time Basket, Emergency Meal Kit Basket, Bath Basket, Stationery Basket, or other basket, as described later in this chapter. Here is a decorating idea:

Bride's Laundry Basket

Stock the basket with a colorful supply of detergents, bleach, spot remover, clothesline and clothespins, spray starch, fabric softener, small wooden drying rack or perhaps an iron or sleeve board. If several of you are serving as hostesses for this party, you can go together on this decoration which is then given to the bride as a gift. Decorate the handles of the basket with ribbons in the wedding colors, of course, along with a few silk flowers.

A SHOWER OF LINENS

Guests should be informed of the bride's bathroom, bedroom and kitchen colors when they are invited to this party.

String a Clothesline

A simple clothesline and a package of colored clothespins serve as the main shower decoration. As the bride opens her gifts (blankets, sheets, towels, etc.), they are hung on this clothesline, along with the accompanying gift card. This idea can be used, on a smaller scale, as a table centerpiece, by using a colored string, toy clothespins and tiny "pretend" towels and blankets that you have made out of sewing scraps. You may want to embroider or use a fabric pen to write the bride's and groom's names on a tiny pair of pillowcases to hang on the line.

LINGERIE SHOWER

This is always a favorite! Guests bring lacy camisoles, sexy nighties, bras and underwear. (Be sure to include the bride's sizes on your invitation.) The clothesline idea works well for this type of shower, too, except that the clothesline centerpiece is hung with tiny black lace bras, panties, etc.

Sexy Mannequin

Borrow or rent a store mannequin to use as your main decoration. Dress her in the sexiest black lingerie you can find, including garter belt and hose. If you can't find an actual store mannequin, use a cardboard cutout instead.

AROUND-THE-CLOCK SHOWER

Here is a chance for your guests to use their creativity! When you send out the party invitations, assign each guest a certain time of day. Each gift should match the assigned time of day; for example, "morning gifts" may include a coffee maker, make-up mirror or alarm clock. "Midday gifts" may include an appointment book, purse, or pen and pencil set. "Evening gifts" can be a bottle of wine, bath oil or a dessert cookbook. See how it works?

Decorated Grandfather Clock

Borrow the tallest grandfather clock you can find to use as your focal decoration. Cover it with fresh or silk flowers, ribbons and other bridal embellishments.

OTHER PARTY THEMES
- Dessert Party
- Bridal Brunch
- Pasta Shower
- A "Roast"
- A Hobby Shower
- A Gourmet Shower
- A "Bon Voyage" Honeymoon Shower

Gifts

Basket Gifts

There were several baskets described in chapter one that are also suitable bridal shower gifts: the Honeymoon Picnic Basket, the Honeymoon Beach Basket, the Love Basket, the

First Home Basket, the Gourmet Coffee Basket, the Soup Basket, and the First Christmas Basket. Here are a few more gift basket ideas:

NEW BRIDE'S "EMERGENCY MEAL KIT" BASKET

For that inevitable night when the couple comes home after work to an empty cupboard and refrigerator, this gift will come in handy. Fill an inexpensive basket with "easy-cooking" food items purchased at your local grocery store: a jar of pre-cooked spaghetti sauce, a package of uncooked spaghetti, a package of bread sticks, canned fruit salad, instant lemonade mix, and a couple of canned ready-to-eat puddings. Line the basket with a small hand towel; add a potholder or wooden mixing spoon. Then wrap it all up in cellophane and tie it with a bow and a card that says: New Bride's Emergency Meal Kit.

CAKE AND COOKIE BASKET

Fill a basket with cake and cookie mixes, packages of chocolate chips and nuts, cake pans, mixing bowls and spoons, potholders, Bundt pan, cake decorating kit, cookie press, electric hand mixer, etc. Top it off with some family recipes handwritten on flowered index cards.

TEA-TIME BASKET

This basket is illustrated on the opening page of this chapter. It is a band box or flowered hat box filled with teapot, cup and saucer, gourmet jams, marmalades and imported tea biscuits. Tuck in tufts of tulle netting, sprigs of delicate silk flowers and lacy ribbons. Tie the entire box, lid and all, with a 1-inch-wide satin acetate ribbon.

BASKET OF FRAGRANCE

Spray paint an old-fashioned Easter basket; line it with lace tablecloth fabric or feminine lace hankies. Fill the basket with potpourri, sachets, colognes, powders, sprays, candles and a small potpourri pot.

SEWING BASKET

If the bride loves to sew, crochet, knit, embroider, cross-stitch or do needlepoint, this is the perfect gift for her. Try to find a basket with a lid so it can be used as an actual sewing basket. Fill it with cross-stitch or needlepoint kits, a small pair of scissors, embroidery threads, a mending kit, a package of needles, yarns, a good "ripper," and other sewing accessories. Tie the basket with a bow made from a measuring tape, along with some colorful silk flowers.

WRITING BASKET

Fill this basket with writing supplies: note paper, thank you notes, feminine stationery, greeting cards, envelopes, stamps, an address book, and several nice pens, including a calligraphy pen. If you know the bride's and groom's future mailing address, order return address stickers to include in this gift basket. Wrap in clear cellophane and tie with a wide gingham bow.

Bride's Emergency
Meal Kit

Towel Bouquet and
Bath Basket

BATH BASKET

Use a can of pink spray paint to liven up any old basket you may have around the house; then line the basket with pink bathroom hand towels or washclothes and fill it with bubble bath, potpourri, perfumed candles, decorator soaps, body gels, powders and sachets. Add a stick of loufa, a bath sponge, and a little scrub brush. Wrap the basket in pink cellophane and tie with a wide, pink satin ribbon.

BASKET BOUQUET

Fashion a basket into a "bouquet" of hand towels and washcloths. Purchase towels and cloths that have satiny, lacy edges; these edges become the "flowers" as each hand towel or washcloth is rolled tightly so they become the "petals" of the flowers in the "bouquet." By the way, you can also create your own satiny, lacy bath linens by merely adding your own trim to plain, less expensive towels and cloths. After you have all the "blooms" facing up, add tiny silk stephanotis and narrow streamers of satin acetate ribbon. The finished look should be that of a bridal bouquet.

BASKET OF LOVE FROM YOUR KITCHEN

Line a basket with 1 square yard of gingham fabric (cut with pinking shears); tuck in a supply of your own homemade jams, jellies, soup mixes, hot spiced tea mixes, biscotti, cookies or breads. Wrap each item in cellophane, tie with ribbon, and add a small card (from your computer or calligraphy pen) that says: "Homemade by Ginny," "With Love From My Kitchen to Yours . . . Ginny" or some other message from you to the bride-to-be. You can add a feminine coffee mug, soup mug, tea ball, cutting board and knife, or a few colorful potholders. Tie the handle of the basket with a gingham bow that matches the gingham liner, along with a set of measuring spoons or a humorous refrigerator magnet.

Other Gift Ideas

There are three gifts described in the first chapter that also make appropriate bridal shower gifts: the Do Not Disturb Sign, Wedding Memorabilia Box and the Keepsake Wedding Pillow. Here are more ideas especially for the bride:

WELCOME TO THE FAMILY BOX

This is a large box filled with colorful cards, one for each "branch of the family tree" that includes the first and last names of each adult and child, their relationships to each other, addresses, telephone numbers, birthdates, wedding anniversaries and directions to each family's home, including maps. Depending on your artistic abilities, you can be as creative as you like with these cards by using a calligraphy pen, adding small photos, or illustrating with drawings or watercolors.

BRIDAL WREATH

Purchase an inexpensive 12- or 14-inch grapevine wreath, a spool of neutral-colored carpet thread, white silk roses or daisies, tiny, delicate accent flowers (such as stephanotis or gypsophila), satin ribbon and several accent items, such as love doves, butterflies or inexpensive gold rings. Place the flowers anywhere on the wreath and attach them by winding them with the carpet thread; continue to add and wind until the grapevine is covered. Then add your ribbon and accent pieces. Use a small piece of 16-gauge floral wire to form a hanging hook on the back of the wreath.

Wreath and Topiary Tree

BRIDAL TOPIARY

These are the supplies you will need to purchase at a craft store in order to make this simple topiary:

- 5-inch Styrofoam ball
- One desert foam brick
- Small bag of natural Spanish moss
- One silk mini-ivy bush
- The same flowers and accent items given above for the Bridal Wreath
- Floral pins
- 4 yards of ¾-inch moire ribbon

- Small package of 18-gauge florist wire
- Hot glue gun or tube of household glue

You will also need a basket (approximately 6 to 8 inches wide) and a natural tree branch about 18 inches long (to be used as the trunk of the topiary tree).

Directions

1. Use glue to secure the desert foam brick snugly in the basket, keeping the foam about ½ inch below the top of the basket.
2. Insert the "tree trunk" about 3 inches into the center of this foam brick.
3. Attach the Styrofoam ball to the top of this tree trunk.
4. Add the Spanish moss around the base of the trunk, filling to the top of the basket.
5. Use the floral pins to attach the flowers, pieces of ivy and accent pieces to the Styrofoam ball.
6. Cut a length of ribbon 3 yards long; starting in the middle, fold the ribbon back and forth, always turning it over in the center so the right side is showing. Then tie the center tightly with florist wire, which will form a bow. Attach this bow to the top of the tree trunk (about 4 inches below the bottom of the Styrofoam ball) by tying with a 9-inch length of the same ribbon.

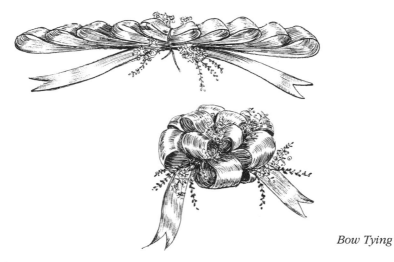

Bow Tying

7. Take the remaining ribbon and cut it into 3-inch lengths; loop these lengths of ribbon and tuck them in between the flowers on the Styrofoam ball. Fasten each loop with floral pins.

Optional: You may add an additional ribbon at the base of the tree trunk, or streamers of narrow ribbon that trail down and around the trunk, a small bird nest settled in between the flowers, or perch a bird on the rim of the basket with one of the ribbon streamers in its beak.

BRIDAL SACHETS

These easy-to-make, inexpensive sachets may be tucked into the bride's honeymoon suitcase, then layered into her lingerie drawer when she gets home. Use the heart pattern shown in chapter one, enlarging to about 8 inches high by 6 inches wide. For each sachet, cut two hearts out of white satin acetate fabric; with right sides facing each other, stitch the two pieces together, leaving a 2-inch opening at the bottom of the heart. Fill the hearts with lavender potpourri, then close each heart by hand-stitching it together at the bottom. Now you're ready to decorate these hearts by adding ruffled lace around the edges, narrow white satin bows, and tiny white seed pearls that may be hot-glued or sewn on by hand.

HONEYMOON BAG

Purchase a large white or pastel makeup bag or small drawstring shoulder bag; fill it with any items you think the bride might need on her honeymoon. Here are some ideas:

- Nail file or emery boards
- Disposable razor
- Clear nail polish
- Nail clippers
- Small pair of scissors
- Emergency mending kit
- Cotton swabs
- Bottle of aspirin
- Under eye concealer
- Lip gloss
- Blemish cream
- Comb
- Bath powder
- Sample-size box of detergent
- Tweezers
- First aid kit
- Sunscreen
- Safety pins

COLANDER SURPRISE!

This ordinary chrome colander is filled with surprises, then tied with cellophane and a bow for a clever, yet affordable, shower gift. Fill the colander with any food or cooking items that relate to pasta dishes, including various types and colors of uncooked pasta, spaghetti sauces, dried tomatoes, spices, parmesan cheese and bread sticks. You can also add a few "extras," such as a pasta spatula, serving ladle, spaghetti measure, or red and white checkered mats, napkins or "bibs."

Filled Colander

By using the ideas in this chapter, your party and gifts will be unique and special because you have created them yourself with love. The bride will sense this love, which will add to her joy as she plans for her wedding!

3

The Rehearsal Dinner

*T*he rehearsal dinner is traditionally a formal, sit-down affair hosted by the groom's parents. However, times have changed, and good, old-fashioned "tradition" has been replaced with "anything goes." Although a formal dinner is still the most popular choice, it may be hosted by any friends or relatives of the bride, or even by the couple themselves.

Whether formal or informal, however, here are a few rules that *should* be followed:

1 Be sure to invite everyone who will be attending the rehearsal, including the clergy, the musicians, the wedding coordinator, all members of the wedding party, including ushers and candlelighters, plus the parents of any children in the wedding and, of course, the parents of the bride and groom. It is also nice, although optional, to invite the nonparticipating spouses or dates of everyone attending the rehearsal, along with any special out-of-town relatives or close friends who have arrived for the wedding. It is also an honor to invite the bride's and groom's grandparents. Mail written invitations to the rehearsal dinner so there aren't any misunderstandings.

2 Be sure to have champagne or nonalcoholic sparkling cider on hand for the toasts, a tradition no matter how silly things get! By the way, the toasts offered at a rehearsal dinner are usually more personal and humorous than those at the wedding reception. This is the normal order of toasts at a rehearsal dinner:

- The best man toasts the couple;
- The groom toasts his bride and her parents;
- The bride toasts her groom and his parents;

- Optional toasts may then be offered by anyone attending the dinner, including other members of the wedding party.

Here is an example of a "personal, humorous toast" given by a groom to the bride's parents: "To Anna's parents, the best Mom and Dad a girl could ever have . . . you can redecorate her room now—I think this is going to work!"

3 The final "must" is to control the alcohol consumption. You can start out with champagne and then, surreptitiously, begin pouring sparkling cider (just wrap a big white, linen napkin around the bottle!). Make it your goal, as host, to "get them to the church on time!"

The Formal Sit-Down Rehearsal Dinner

The formality of an elegant sit-down dinner is the preferred celebration following the rehearsal, and it's usually hosted by the groom's parents. In addition to the three rules just explained, you'll want to follow other rules of etiquette as well.

FORMAL TABLE SEATING

There are traditional rules of protocol when it comes to rehearsal dinner seating. Here is one common arrangement for seating around two long tables. Other guests and ceremony participants may be seated randomly at the remaining tables.

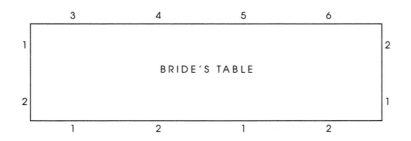

1 Bridesmaids
2 Groomsmen
3 Best Man
4 Bride
5 Groom
6 Maid/Matron of Honor

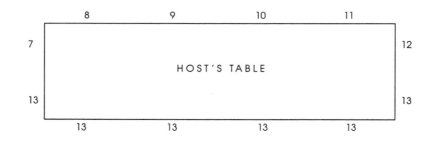

7 Father-of-the-Bride
8 Mother-of-the-Bride
9 Father-of-the-Groom (Host)
10 Mother-of-the-Groom (Hostess)
11 Clergy
12 Clergy's Spouse
13 Other Relatives or Guests

Decorating the Tables

TABLE LINENS

Use the real thing: No paper! Fine linen cloths and napkins set an exquisite tone, either in white or a color to complement your china. The two-tiered cloth is another elegant choice; you can create your own by placing a piece of solid-colored fabric underneath a lace tablecloth. The napkins should match and be folded in such a way that they "make a statement." By folding your napkins in a distinctive way, you can turn an ordinary table into a spectacular one. Here are several napkin-folding ideas:

Rolled With a Ribbon

Fold the napkin in half and then roll it up long ways starting at the narrow end of the folded napkin; tie it in the center with a ribbon.

Fan-folded With a Ribbon

Fold the napkin back and forth, creasing as you go, to form a fan. Tie the "fan" with a bow near the bottom. (See the illustration on the opening page of this chapter.)

Fan-folded Into a Goblet

Fold the napkin in half, then fan-fold it back and forth. Place the napkin "stem" down into a goblet; the napkin will flair up like a flower petal.

Rolled Napkins

Bow-Tied Spoon

Fan-Folded Napkin

CHINA, CRYSTAL AND SILVER

This is the time to set your table with the finest china, crystal and silver you can find. If you don't own the "real thing," you can always rent it from a party rental store or borrow from Mom or other relatives. If you end up with various china patterns from several sources, don't worry because that's very chic these days. Mix the patterns on one table, or set each table with its own matching patterns. In any case, show them off with special touches, such as tying a ribbon around the end of a spoon; then placing the spoon in the cup on its saucer sitting in the middle of the place setting.

PLACE CARDS
Gold Truffle Boxes

Use the box pattern in chapter one to make these elegant place cards (or purchase pre-cut boxes in lots of fifty, costing about eighteen cents per box). After you've assembled a box for each guest, spray the boxes with gold paint. Make or purchase chocolate truffles; place two in each box. Wrap the boxes with white ribbons and top off with pure white place cards, calligraphied with each guest's name. Place a box above each guest's dinner plate.

Personalized Picture Frames

Purchase tiny, stand-up picture frames, one for each guest. Write or calligraphy the guests' names onto white linen paper cut to fit inside the frames. Set the frames above each guest's place setting.

Personalized Napkin Rings

Save all your cardboard tubes from rolls of wax paper, toilet paper, wrapping paper and shelf paper. Cut them into 3-inch lengths and cover them with white satin acetate fabric. (Each piece of fabric should be about 7 inches long by 5 inches wide.) Spray glue to the inside and outside of the 3-inch cardboard tube, then wrap the 5-inch width of fabric around the tube, stuffing the ends of the fabric inside the tube. After the napkin holders are dry, use a black liquid embroidery pen to write each guest's name in the center of a holder. Fold each napkin back and forth (into a fan shape) and pull it through the napkin holder. Place a napkin, with its personalized holder, in the center of each plate.

Bud Vase at Each Place

Buy tiny bud vases, one for each guest. Fill them with tight rosebuds; thread a narrow, satin acetate ribbon through a hole punched in a white place card with the guest's name written in black (you can make these on your computer using a fancy font). Tie the ribbon (with place card attached) to the lower stem of the rosebud. Set a vase in the center of each guest's plate.

Wedding Bell Place Cards

Use the pattern below to cut out your own wedding bell place cards. Use lightweight white poster board or heavy white linen paper; write the guests' names on the front of the bells. Fold the bell at the dotted line and set at the top of each guest's place setting.

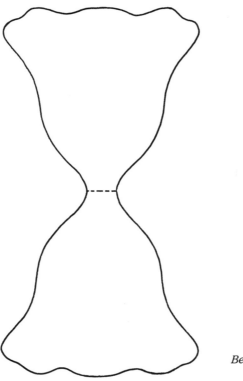

Bell Place Card Pattern

FAVORS

The first four place card ideas given above will also serve as favors. Here are five more favor ideas:

Tied Mints

I'm almost embarrassed to give you this idea because it's so simple, and yet it's an idea that works every time! Buy a large box of thin chocolate mints, already individually wrapped. Divide them into stacks of three mints each; tie each stack with a narrow satin ribbon and place at each place setting.

Wrapped Champagne Splits

Buy cases of champagne splits (each equals about one-fourth of a regular bottle); wrap each split in gold cellophane, tied at the neck with a piece of gold ribbon.

Tiny Boxes of Pastel Mints

Use the box pattern in chapter one or purchase pre-cut boxes (about eighteen cents each). Spray them any color you wish; and fill with six or eight pastel mints. Tie the box with a ribbon.

Lace Doily Tussie Mussie

Wrap a 4-inch doily around a single flower; tie it tightly with a ribbon.

Tussie Mussie Favor

Mini Wedding Wreaths

Purchase 2-inch grapevine wreaths; wind narrow white satin ribbon around each wreath, leaving space between each wrap; fill these spaces with dried white gypsophila; tie a bow at the top of each wreath, using the same white satin ribbon.

CENTERPIECES

A centerpiece is the focal point of any table and should complement the style and colors of your china and linens. At a rehearsal dinner it is important for each table to be conducive to conversation, because there may be members of the bride's and groom's families who are meeting for the first time. Keep your centerpieces nice and low so all the guests have eye contact. These "centers of interest" should also be eye-appealing and special, in addition to being affordable. Fortunately, this is an easy task; all you need are some good ideas:

Candles and Mirrors

Run a ribbon 4 inches in width across the table, extending to the edges of the tablecloth. Place one or more mirrors flat in the center of the table and place five to seven votive candles on the mirrors, tying each holder with lengths of narrow ribbon that match the wider ribbon used as a runner. Place single flowers (live or silk), plus evergreen sprigs around the base of each votive candle.

Miniature Topiaries

Place some floral foam in the bottom of a 3-inch clay flowerpot; cut a 10-inch branch from a tree (preferably a willow tree) to be used as the "trunk" of the topiary. Press the branch about 1½ inches into the floral foam. Use floral pins to cover a 3-inch Styrofoam ball with dried Spanish moss; then press the top of the branch (trunk) about 1½ inches into the ball. Using a hot glue gun, cover the ball with dried flowers that complement your color scheme; accent the ball with dried white gypsophila. Now you're ready for the finishing touches: wrap the pot with any fabric of your choice (moire, brocade, taffeta, tulle netting, etc.) and tie with a ribbon at the base of the "trunk." Add small ribbons to the ball of flowers, letting the ends trail down. Set these mini-topiaries in beds of greenery from your garden or in swirls of tulle netting.

Antique China Arrangements

Let your containers be the focal points. Use antique gravy boats, teapots, or cups with saucers as your flower "vases." Arrange fresh or silk flowers in each container. By using these exquisite pieces, inexpensive do-it-yourself bouquets become stunning centerpieces.

Evergreens and Dried Herbs

Cut sprigs of small-patterned evergreens, such as boxwood, juniper or Korean holly and arrange them in circular or oblong clusters in the center of your table. Add dried herbs, such as sage, rosemary or lavender, along with two or three colorful silk or fresh flowers. Top off with narrow ribbon bows, with long knotted streamers.

Candlestick With Floral Wreath

Purchase inexpensive, foam-filled floral adapters for your candlesticks; these adapters can be filled with dried herbs and flowers, forming a wreath where the candle meets the candlestick. Use one as a centerpiece, or cluster three together (in varying heights).

Hurricane Chimneys on Mirrors

Place a clear glass hurricane chimney over a single candle standing on a round mirror; surround the chimney with evergreen sprigs and ribbon bows. Or, you can wrap the base of the chimney in gold lamé fabric covered with white tulle netting. Tie the top of the chimney with ½-inch-wide gold glitter ribbon, tied into a simple bow, but with very long ends that trail, twirl and spiral around the entire table top.

Wine Glasses on Mirrors

Gather an uneven number of wine glasses in assorted shapes and heights; arrange them on a mirror. Fill the wine glasses with dried herbs or tiny silk flowers and trailing ribbons.

Tied Evergreens, Candlestick and Hurricane Chimney

Cake Pedestal and Figurine

Use a simple cake pedestal plate as a base, and add any appropriate figurine (such as a cherub or love doves). Surround the figurine with wide lace ribbon and single rosebuds, daisies or any silk or fresh flowers you have available.

Reaffirmation Centerpiece

The formality of this type of elegant dinner party creates the perfect ambiance for the reaffirmation of wedding vows. If any of the parents' or grandparents' wedding anniversaries happen to fall close to this event, especially a twenty-fifth or fiftieth, this is the time and place for them to reaffirm their vows. The real beauty of this idea is that your table decor will be provided for you, and at no cost! Just ask the couple(s) for framed wedding photos and any small memorabilia that can be used as centerpieces. (Be sure to provide plenty of tissues because there may be some tears!)

Bride Doll Centerpiece

Doll collecting has become a very popular hobby. See if you can borrow enough bride dolls to have one for every table at your dinner. (In a pinch, you can use Barbie bride dolls.) Swirl tulle netting at the brides' feet, with tiny rosebuds (live or silk) tucked into the netting

Informal Rehearsal Dinners

Informal rehearsal dinners don't require fine linens, crystal or china, and they don't require favors or elegant centerpieces. Here are some of today's easy and relaxed alternatives to the formal sit-down dinner, along with a few decorating gimmicks:

PICNIC IN THE PARK
Helium Balloons

At the end of the picnic, release as many helium balloons as you can afford, each printed with the bride's and groom's names. You can purchase a disposable cannister of helium at a discount department store for about fifteen dollars—enough to fill at least twenty-five balloons or you can rent a helium tank for thirty-five dollars, enough to fill two hundred balloons.

HORS D'OEUVRES AND CHAMPAGNE BESIDE THE POOL
Floating Rafts

Fill several small rafts with flowers, greenery and ribbons in the wedding colors. If it's warm enough to party around the pool, it's probably the right time of year to "beg, borrow and steal" colorful blooms from your friends', neighbors' and co-hosts' gardens!

CAKE AND COFFEE IN SOMEONE'S HOME
A Personalized Cake

If you're only serving cake and coffee, why not have a little fun with it? With the help of your favorite bakery, design a personalized cake, such as one that includes baby pictures of the bride and groom, or decorations relating to their hobbies. (A tiny soccer ball? A miniature tennis racket? A little, red "hot car"?) Use your imagination!

POTLUCK SUPPER
Fancy Recipe Cards

Furnish fancy recipe cards to each cook who will provide a dish for this potluck dinner. Then display the corresponding recipe card beside each dish. Let the cooks "show off" a little with their traditional family favorites. The couple can take these recipe cards with them to try out after the honeymoon, as well as a remembrance of the occasion.

BACKYARD BARBECUE
Show and Tell

Since a barbecue is already a "roast" of sorts, why not have several friends and family members "show" (using family photos, home movies, videos, or childhood treasures belonging to the bride and groom) or "tell" about silly or embarrassing incidents in the lives of the couple? Warn your family and friends ahead of time so they can be digging up old photos or mementos and recalling things that were said or done.

OTHER INFORMAL PARTY IDEAS
- Beer and pizza on the patio
- Buffet brunch
- Beach party
- Ethnic heritage party
- Dutch treat at a restaurant

There are also three themes presented in chapter one that can be adapted for an informal rehearsal party: Country-Western, Nostalgia and Polynesian.

The informal rehearsal dinner is not as stiff as the more formal affair, and it's usually quite festive, fun and high-spirited as well. Many families like to laugh and get a little silly after the rehearsal; they think it helps everyone relax for the big day ahead. They just may be right!

4

The Ceremony

*T*he overall tone for your ceremony will be determined by several factors: Number of guests? Civil or religious? Degree of formality? Type of site? If you're getting married underwater while scuba diving, you obviously won't worry about elaborate pew bows, and if you're going to stand barefoot in a field of wildflowers, a la the sixties, there's no need to fret over your shoes! But if you're getting married in a more conventional setting, such as a church, synagogue, club hall, home or garden, you'll be able to use most of the ideas in this chapter. Whether decorating the site or the wedding party itself, you can save hundreds of dollars by employing a few do-it-yourself ideas with professional looking results!

Themes

Why do you need a theme? You don't, but it will certainly make your wedding easier to plan. It's a lot of fun, too, as you carry your theme throughout, from the invitations, to the pew arrangements, to the garlands on the windows, to the ribbons on the candle sconces, to the women's bouquets, the men's boutonnieres, and the flower girl's basket. You see, your theme will create the mood that ties everything together.

Here are a few theme ideas to whet your appetite:

WREATHS

Incorporate decorated Styrofoam or grapevine wreaths of different sizes. Hang them high on each side of the altar, on the pews, pillars, windows and candelabra. Also, your bridesmaids and flower girl can carry wreaths decorated with fresh or silk flowers.

BELLS

Use tissue-fold bells of various sizes; they are available in many colors, but you will probably want to use white or gold for your ceremony site. They can be worked into all your decorations; tie them with ribbons in your wedding colors.

DOUBLE RINGS

Gold rings of various sizes incorporated into the invitations, pew arrangements, bouquets, flower girl's basket, candelabra flowers, etc.

VALENTINE'S

Red hearts, flowers, ribbons, candles, dresses, cummerbunds and bow ties, along with plenty of cupids with their bows and arrows.

CANDLELIGHT

For an evening wedding, use candles every way possible, from pillar sconces, to candelabra, to windowsills, to the altar railing, to the ends of the pews, and the top of the organ. The bridal attendants can each carry a candle imbedded in an oasis filled with fresh flowers, and you may want to include a traditional unity candle.

LOVE DOVES

Doves everywhere, from the pew arrangements to the candelabra to the garlands along the altar, trailing ribbons from their beaks.

RENAISSANCE

You can take this theme as far as you want by sending invitations on rolled parchment, selecting velvet or brocade gowns for the bride and her attendants, and including music played on a mandolin, lyre or harpsichord.

VICTORIAN

You'll need to include hearts, lace, roses, trailing ribbons, fans, nosegays or tussie mussies. The bride and her attendants may want to wear bustled, high-necked gowns and high-buttoned shoes.

SOUTHERN PLANTATION

Here is your chance to play Scarlett for a day! Get out the hoopskirts and parasols for you and your attendants, along with the ruffled shirts and string ties for the men. Use trellised arbors and magnolia branches to recreate the ambiance of an antebellum garden.

ETHNIC

Many of us are from mixed cultural backgrounds, but if you have a strong ethnic heritage, incorporate it into your wedding theme. Use ethnic costumes as the basic design for your gown and attendants' dresses, and incorporate the colors from your country's flag. Include any traditional wedding customs. For example, Polish brides wear embroidered white aprons over their wedding gowns, and Mexican and Filipino couples drape white silk chords over their shoulders to proclaim their union. Chinese brides wear red wedding gowns, Finnish brides wear golden crowns, and French bridesmaids carry fans. What precious traditions!

BLACK AND WHITE WEDDING

This is a popular nineties theme: the bride wears white, of course, and the men wear black tuxes. The attendants wear black dresses with white trim, each dress in a little different style. The flower girl wears white and the ring bearer wears a black tuxedo.

SNOWBALL WEDDING

Everyone wears white! Even the mothers and grandmothers of the bride and groom. The trick with this wedding theme is to have *all* the whites match. If some of the whites are ivory, some are cream, and some are "blue-white," the off-whites will appear to be dirty, so start with the bride's gown and match every white to that of her dress. Use bright, vibrant colors in the flowers and decorations. (This will emphasize the stark beauty of the white.)

CHRISTMAS

Use reds and greens, along with accents of white. The bridal attendants can wear cranberry red with white fur muffs; the bride's bouquet may be composed of holly and poinsettias; the flower girl might carry a holly wreath. Use strands of tiny white Christmas tree lights and white candles to illuminate an evening wedding.

COUNTRY

Here is your chance to use those light, airy fabrics, such as dotted Swiss, organdy, eyelet or checked gingham. Decorate with hand-tied wildflowers, sheaves of wheat or nosegays of herbs. Include white wicker, trellises, arches and gazebos, especially if the wedding will be held outdoors.

Wedding Invitations

You can design your own original, personalized invitations by creating a master that can be copied at a quick-print shop. If you have access to a laser printer or a quality ink-jet printer (at least 600×300 dpi), you can make a master by using a fancy font on a computer, or you might want to have a master drawn up by a calligrapher.

Have the master copied onto blank wedding invitations purchased from a paper supply store. They come in sets that include the invitation, an inner and outer envelope and tissue inserts. Here is sample wording for your invitation:

Mr. and Mrs. Edwin Collins

request the honour of your presence

at the marriage of their daughter

Anna Marie

to

John Brian Garner

Saturday the ninth of April

Nineteen hundred and ninety four

at seven o'clock in the evening

Church by the Wayside

12 Greenwood Avenue

Pleasanton, Georgia

Browse through the wedding stationery catalogs at your local stationery stores or bridal salons for more contemporary wording that can be used to customize your invitations.

Ceremony Programs

I only see ceremony programs at about half the weddings I attend; however, here are five good reasons to furnish them to your guests:

1. The program gives the order of the service.
2. Each participant in the wedding is listed as well as their relationship to the bride or groom.
3. Any special inclusions in the ceremony can be explained, such as a floral wreath in honor of a deceased family member, an ethnic custom, or the fact that the bride is wearing her grandmother's wedding gown and veil.
4. The program provides a way to publicly thank those who helped with the wedding.
5. A program will become a treasured memento of the ceremony.

The ceremony program can be composed on a word processor using any cursive or fancy font, then printed onto parchment or fine linen paper. Once printed, the program can be rolled into a scroll and secured with an ornamental gold ring, or folded and tied at the fold with a narrow satin ribbon.

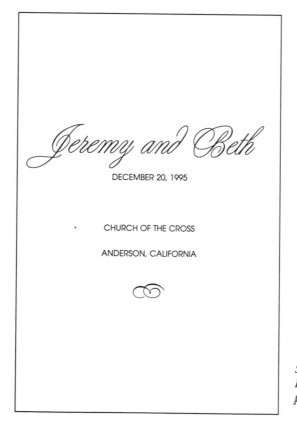

Sample Ceremony Program
page 1 of 4

Wedding Party

Parents of the Bride and Groom

Mr. and Mrs. Robert Collins, Sr.

Mr. and Mrs. William Henderson

Maid of Honor	Nancy Collins	Sister of the bride
Best Man	Gary Costello	Friend of the groom
Bridesmaids	Rachel Johnson	Friend of the bride
	Michelle Henderson	Sister of the groom
	Sara Little	Friend of the bride
Groomsmen	Russ Little	Friend of the groom
	Michael Peterson	Brother-in-law of the groom
	Thomas Garrow	Friend of the groom
Flower Girls	Belinda Jameson	Niece of the bride
	Ashley Stone	Friend of the bride
Ringbearer	Timothy Henson	Nephew of the groom
Candlelighters	Susan Thomas	Friend of the bride
	Pat Cunningham	Friend of the bride and groom
Officiants	Dr. John Hampton	Pastor of Church of the Cross
	Pastor Darren Ell~~~~	Cousin of the groom
Musicians	Clara Alderson	
	Bruce Tilson	
	Craig Holbrook	

Order of Service

Prelude	Christmas Favorites
Candlelighting	"Jesu, Joy of Man's Desiring"
Seating of Honored Guests	"Ave Maria"

Lighting of Memorial Candle and
Seating of Mother of the Bride

Processional	"Trumpet Voluntary"

Giving of the Bride

Prayer

Reading Scripture

Pastoral Address

Exchanging of vows and rings

Lighting of Unity Candle*

Pronouncement of Marriage

Introduction of the bride and groom

Jumping of the broom*

Recessional	"Mendelssohn's Wedding

The memorial candle is in loving memory of
Esther Collins, grandmother of the bride

*The Unity Candle symbolizes the
unity of the bride and groom as they leave
their families and become one.

*The jumping of the broom is an African-American
wedding tradition that demonstrates the sweeping
away of the old life and the starting of
a new life of commitment to each other.

Special Thanks to. . .

Marvin Hollister
for helping us share our wedding with those
who couldn't be here.

Eleanor Hanson
for her loving help coordinating our wedding.

Decorating the Site

As you consider the following decorating ideas, keep your theme in mind. For example, if you decide on a Country theme, you may want to use checked gingham fabric for any bows included in the decor, or if you choose a Victorian wedding, dried herbs may be appropriate whenever possible. If you want your wedding to have a distinctly original look, as opposed to the same old "cookie cutter" thing we so often see, use the ideas in this chapter to trigger your very own "never-heard-of-before-completely-new-and-novel" decorations! Say to yourself, "I'm going to give our guests something to talk about!"

Wedding Flowers

There are many questions to consider when selecting your wedding flowers: Fresh or silk? Cost? What flowers are in season? Formal or informal arrangements? Colors? Size of the blooms? The flowers' meanings? Evening wedding? Suitability to your theme? When I mention "theme," you probably wouldn't select Bird of Paradise, for example, if your theme is Country. And you certainly don't want a lot of fussy, tussie-mussie-type herbal arrangements if your wedding has a sophisticated Black and White theme. If the church has high ceilings, use tall arrangements; if an evening wedding, use white or light-colored flowers.

The formality of your wedding will be a factor, as well. If formal or very formal, the flowers are usually white, lavish and elegant. If semi-formal or informal, there are many options: baskets of cut flowers, wreaths, a hat brimming with blooms, flowering plants, simple bouquets and floral arrangements.

Here are the traditional meanings of some of the most popular wedding flowers: Apple blossoms—Good fortune; Bachelor's button—Hope; Bluebell—Constancy; Blue violet—Faithfulness; Carnation—Pure, deep love; Forget-me-not—Do not forget me; Gardenia—Joy; Honeysuckle—Fidelity; Iris—Good health; Ivy—Good luck; Jasmine—Grace, elegance; Lilac—First love; Lily—Purity; Lily of the valley—Happiness; Magnolia—Love of nature; Myrtle—Affection; Orange blossoms—Purity; Rose—Love; Rosemary—Fidelity; White daisy—Innocence.

Pews and Pillars

TULLE BOWS AND GARLANDS
Materials
- Tulle netting, cut into pieces 18 inches wide by 3 yards long
- Satin acetate ribbon, 2¾ inches wide
- *Optional:* Silk flowers and greenery

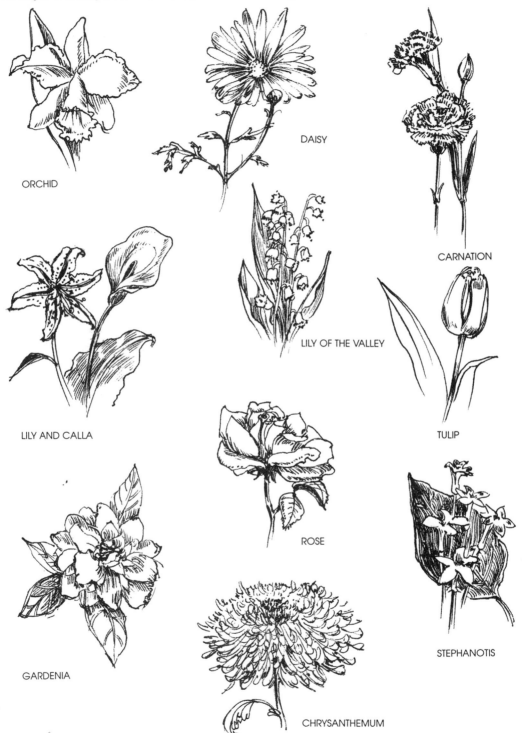

ORCHID

DAISY

CARNATION

LILY AND CALLA

LILY OF THE VALLEY

TULIP

ROSE

GARDENIA

CHRYSANTHEMUM

STEPHANOTIS

Popular Wedding Flowers

- *Optional*: Novelty theme decorations, such as bells, doves, etc.
- Masking tape, 3 inches wide

Instructions

Double the pieces of netting lengthwise. Tie each piece into a large, single bow, leaving the ends streaming down. Tape the bow to the pew using the masking tape. Add a smaller satin acetate bow under each tulle bow. *Optional*: Add sprigs of silk greenery or flowers, plus novelty theme decorations.

WREATHS
Materials

- 12- or 14-inch Styrofoam or grapevine wreaths
- Dried herbs
- Dried white gypsophila
- Silk ivy
- Fabric or ribbon of your choice
- Plastic pew hangers

Instructions

Decorate the wreaths with the flowers, herbs and ivy. Tie the ribbon or fabric strips into a bow at the top of each wreath and hang on pew hangers.

DECORATED CANDLESTICKS
Materials

- 6-foot pew candlesticks (rent from a florist or party rental store)
- Satin acetate ribbon, 2¾ inches wide
- Tulle netting, cut into pieces 2 yards long by 3 inches wide
- Silk ivy, 6-foot lengths
- Silk rosebushes, one per candlestick
- Candles, 14 inches tall, one per candlestick
- Florist wire, lightweight

Instructions

Place one candlestick at each pew or at every other pew. Tie the satin acetate ribbon into 5-yard bows (see chapter two for instructions). Attach a bow to each candlestick at base of candle, leaving long trailing ends that touch the floor. Attach five lengths of tulle netting per candlestick, securing under each bow. Attach the ivy, securing to the top of the candlestick with lightweight florist wire. Cut the roses off the bush; wire six or seven roses to each strand of ivy, spacing them at even intervals from the base of the candle to the floor.

EVERGREEN BOUGHS

If you have free access to evergreen trees, you can decorate the pews very inexpensively.

Materials

- Boughs cut from evergreen trees, about 18 inches long
- Satin acetate ribbon, 2¾ inches wide, or fabric of your choice
- Dried white gypsophila *or*
- White silk stephanotis
- *Optional:* Novelty theme decorations, such as bells, doves, etc.
- Florist wire, medium weight
- Masking tape, 3 inches wide

Instructions

Cluster evergreen boughs together until each spray is about 12 inches wide. Wire the boughs together at the cut ends. Tie a 5-yard bow out of the ribbon, leaving the ends long enough to trail to the bottom of the evergreen spray (or tie a single bow from a piece of fabric cut 5 inches wide by 2 yards long).

Tape the bough securely to the pew, then tape the bow over the top of the spray so it covers the cut ends of the evergreen boughs. Embellish with the stephanotis or gypsophila and the novelty decorations.

FLORAL CASCADES WITH FABRIC BOWS

Materials

- Any fabric that coordinates with your wedding theme: checked gingham, organdy, taffeta, brocade, chintz, etc. cut into strips 8 inches wide
- Flowers of your choice, either silk or fresh; allow eight to twenty-four flowers per pew depending on the size of the flowers
- Filler greens (holly, ivy, evergreenery, etc.)
- Floral tape
- Florist wire, medium weight
- *Optional:* Lace or eyelet ruffled trim for bows
- *Optional:* Novelty theme decorations, such as bells, doves, etc.

Instructions

Hem the raw edges of the fabric ribbons, trimming with the optional lace or eyelet ruffles; tie into single bows. Iron the fabric strips, using heavy starch for body. If using fresh flowers, mix them with the filler greens, then tape and wire them securely at the stems (by taping first, then wiring on top of the tape, you will prevent cutting through the tender stems). If using silk flowers, add the filler greens, then wire together tightly at stems.

Using the masking tape, secure the flowers and greenery to the pew with stems facing *up*. Add the bows, covering the stems. Add any optional novelty decorations.

FULL FLORAL BOUQUETS

Materials

- Flowers of your choice, either silk or fresh; allow eight to twenty-four flowers per pew depending on the size of the flowers
- Filler greens, as above
- Satin acetate ribbon, 1 inch wide
- Pew floral hangers (for fresh or silk flowers)

Instructions

The big difference between this pew arrangement and the one just described above, is that these flowers stand upright with the blooms extending 3 to 6 inches above the pew. If using fresh flowers, place them in the watered oasis floral holders, adding greenery for fullness. If using silk flowers, place them in the foam floral holders, also adding greenery for fullness. Tie a double bow out of the satin acetate ribbon and attach it to the base of the floral holder, letting long ends trail and spiral down the side of the pew.

This is one of the most opulent looks I've ever seen used. If the arrangements are ordered through a florist, the total expense can become exorbitant; however, if you have access to fresh flowers cut from your own garden or donated by friends and relatives, the cost will be minimal.

The Front of the Ceremony Site

EVERGREEN GARLANDS

Evergreen garlands probably give more bang for the buck than anything I know. They cost practically nothing to assemble and yet they fill many spaces, including pews, railings, staircases, arbors, altars, doorways, window frames, tables, candelabra, trellises, walls and tables. You can assemble these garlands several days in advance; simply spray them with mist, wrap in plastic and store in a cool place.

Materials

- Evergreen boughs, cut into 6- or 8-inch lengths
- Floral wire, medium weight
- Satin acetate ribbon, 1 inch wide *or*
- Fabric, cut into 1-inch strips
- *Optional:* Dried herbs or silk flowers

Instructions

Bunch several lengths of evergreen cuttings together in your hand, stems together; wrap them with floral wire. Add a second bunch of greens, overlapping the first lengths by about 3 inches; wire the stems of the second bunch onto the first. Continue this process until your garland is the desired length. After each garland is in its place, add bows, trailing ribbons and any optional herbs or flowers.

These garlands can also be swagged from pew to pew along the inside aisle, giving your pew arrangements an added look of opulence. If your wedding is being held in a large sanctuary that holds several hundred people, but you only expect a hundred or so guests, these garlands can also be used on the outside aisles along the rear pews. This will force your guests to sit in the forward pews or chairs, which will feel better for everyone, including the guests themselves.

POTTED PLANTS, SHRUBS AND TREES

Rent or borrow as much of this greenery as you can find; they make great "fillers" for the front of your church or hall.

Many nurseries will loan out a designated number of potted plants, bushes or trees for a local wedding; some rent them. In our daughter's case, a local nursery gave us a choice of any twelve potted plants or trees, at no charge, as long as we returned them undamaged.

Your family and friends probably own dozens of potted plants or trees, as well, such as silk ficus trees, live philodendron plants and potted camelia bushes. You'll be pleasantly surprised to see how this greenery will help fill large, gaping spaces on a platform or around the altar.

ARBORS, TRELLISES AND WHITE PICKET FENCES

You usually think of using these at a garden wedding, but many brides like to bring the garden inside. In fact, it has become quite popular to convert an ordinary interior setting into a garden by borrowing or renting white arbors, trellises and picket fences. Using the free or borrowed "fillers" mentioned above, create a garden right inside the church or hall! Wind silk ivy and flowers, or live magnolia branches around these props; then add live potted chrysanthemums, miniature roses or marguerite bushes.

WALL WREATHS

Purchase two Styrofoam or grapevine wreaths, the largest you can find, to hang high on the right and left walls in the front of your site. I happen to live in wine country, so many brides in my area gather up dead grapevines at pruning time and form them into giant wreaths (8 feet wide!). They wind them with wide satin acetate or fabric ribbon, leaving space in between the wraps, then tying into a large bow off center at the bottom or top of the wreath. If you use Styrofoam, wind in the same way, but cover the entire wreath; add a 10-yard bow made out of 2¾-inch ribbon, along with silk or fresh flowers and ivy.

Garlands

Trellis Chupah

CANDLES, CANDLES, CANDLES!

The use of candles is another relatively economical way to decorate a ceremony site. By filling the front of the church with candelabra, you won't need to provide as many flowers. Borrow or rent six- or eight-tiered candelabra; arrange them on the platform or behind the altar. Decorate each one with silk or fresh flowers, "filler greens," such as ivy, holly or evergreen boughs, and 10-yard bows tied out of 4-inch ribbons.

You can also add candles as pew decorations, as already mentioned, or on candle sconces mounted on all the side pillars, columns or walls of the room. The sconces can be decorated using many of the same ideas already given for pew decorations. Covering the candles with hurricane chimneys will add drama, as well. Single candles also can be added to the top of the organ or piano or along the railing in front of the altar.

SWAGS OF TULLE NETTING

You can achieve a striking effect with the use of tulle netting. It is amazingly inexpensive (about $1.19 per yard), so you don't need to skimp! In fact, you'll probably want to purchase one or two entire bolts to swag, tie and drape about. It can be used to swag from pillar to pillar or pew to pew or over doorways or windows. I have seen it used as the focal decoration on the wall behind the altar by tying the "swags" with ribbons that are held in the beaks of oversized white doves. The ribbon can be tied randomly or at the upper right and left corners of the swag. *Optional:* Use silk flowers in place of the doves.

AFFORDABLE FLORAL ARRANGEMENTS

Many party rental stores will rent a pair of white wicker baskets filled with white silk gladioluses and chrysanthemums for about forty dollars a pair. The flowers are full and realistic and, along with the basket, stand about 5 feet tall. All you need to add are a couple of 10-yard bows.

Another economical idea is to fill your own oversized vases with flowering shrubs, magnolia branches, orange or almond blossoms, or cut flowers from your own garden. If the wedding is in the spring, lilacs are an excellent choice because they're not only easy to arrange, but they fill the entire room with their fragrance.

Other options are to order your arrangements from a supermarket florist, which will save you 50 to 75 percent off regular retail, or from a wholesale flower mart.

CHRISTMAS TREE LIGHTS

Borrow as many strings of tiny white Christmas lights as you can find; use them to decorate "filler" plants and trees, garlands, wreaths and any other decorations in the room. Of course, this idea works best for an evening wedding.

THE CHUPAH

If you are having a Jewish wedding, you will be required to provide a chupah, a small canopy that stands in the front of the synagogue. It must be large enough to at least shelter the bride and groom during the ceremony; however, if it is quite large, others may stand under it as well: the rabbi, the cantor and the parents of the couple. If your synagogue doesn't provide a chupah for wedding ceremonies, here are two affordable ideas:

1 Form the four corners of the chupah by mounting 10-foot poles (plain or cut from tree branches) firmly into Christmas tree stands. Make a delicate, airy white canopy cover out of fabric hand embroidered by several family members or from purchased tablecloth fabric. You may also use a family heirloom for this purpose, or the prayer shawl worn by the groom at his bar mitzvah. Use narrow white ribbon to tie the corners of the cloth to the tops of the four poles. The poles may be sprayed gold or decorated with ribbons and flowers. The tree stands may be covered with swirls of white tulle netting decorated with tiny ribbons and silk or fresh flowers.

2 Cover a large, arched arbor with greenery, tulle netting and fresh or silk flowers. If you decide to decorate this trellis chupah with fresh flowers, it's a good idea to hide small water tubes among the greenery so the flowers will stay fresh throughout the ceremony.

"Decorating" the Wedding Party

The Bride's Headpiece and Veil

Although the bride's headpiece and veil end up as one piece, they are purchased and assembled separately. By making your own, you can literally save hundreds of dollars. I have a headpiece and veil that I use in my wedding seminars that I made for less than $20. It is a copy of one I saw in a bridal salon for $175! Mine was even featured on CNN's "Daywatch" TV program, which is pretty amazing to me since I made the whole thing without a pattern one evening while I was watching "Cheers." Believe me, you can do it, too! Even if you don't sew anything else for your wedding, you should consider making your headpiece and veil. A veil requires a minimum of talent and expense, and the potential cost savings are enormous!

Before launching into this project, however, it's a good idea to try on several ready-made headpieces and veils so you'll know what style is most flattering to your face and features. While you're at it, sneak a peek at their simple construction; this will encourage you to try your hand at making your own.

By the way, if your wedding gown is quite detailed and frilly, it will look best with a very simple headpiece and veil. However, if your dress has plain lines and is unadorned, your headpiece and veil should be more intricate and "fussy." Your gown and headpiece should never fight each other for attention.

HEADPIECES

Covered Frames

There are several popular styles of headpiece frames: camelot, cap, Juliet, band and wreath. You can purchase these frames, already covered in fabric, from your local fabric store; uncovered wire frames are available through catalogs and craft stores. I recommend, however, that you purchase a covered frame because they aren't that much more expensive, will save time, and are ready to decorate by adding lace, trim, beads, sequins, silk flowers or pearls, all with the help of your trusty glue gun! Once the glue has dried, you're ready to add your veil.

Hats

You can also start with a simple hat and embellish it with ribbons and silk flowers, or by adding a veil. The three most popular hat styles are the derby, the picture hat and the pillbox. You can purchase basic bridal wedding hats at your wedding supply store or at many fabric stores. You also can use a wide-brimmed straw hat, which can be sprayed white using a can of flat enamel paint spray.

Flower or Bow

A simple silk flower or bow is one of the most inexpensive ideas of all. You will need to secure the flower(s) or bow to a small comb; use heavy drapery thread. My twenty dollar veil creation started with two silk flowers, already wired and satin wrapped, that I purchased from a wedding supply store. I merely bent them into a "headband" and sewed them to a small clear plastic comb. You may decide to use a silk flower in addition to a bow.

Crowns or Tiaras

You can purchase crowns or tiaras in a variety of styles and prices from a wedding supply store or from one of those accessory shops you find at the malls. They are usually ornamented with pearls or rhinestones.

VEILS

The bridal veil originated back in the days when a man and woman were matched for marriage without having seen each other. The bride arrived at her wedding wearing a veil that concealed her face completely; the groom was never allowed to "unveil" her until after they were already married. This tradition has evolved through the years as the veil became thinner and, eventually, didn't necessarily cover the face at all.

The two most common veil fabrics are Illusion Nylon and Tulle Netting. The Illusion is the finer fabric of the two because it is soft, delicate and drapeable. The tulle is a little thicker and is usually used for the attendants' headpieces. Another important advantage of the Illusion fabric is that it comes in wide widths—72, 108 and 144 inches; the tulle usually comes in a 54-inch width. By using the Illusion fabric your veil can be wider without any piecing. These veil fabrics are very affordable so you might as well copy the more costly ready-made veils by doubling your fabric. This will make your veil appear "whiter" and "heavier" and "more expensive," especially if you're doubling 144-inch-wide Illusion fabric.

Most veil styles don't need a pattern, only simple guidelines for shape and dimensions. One word of advice: Always cut your veil fabric *longer* than you think you'll want; you can always shorten it after you've finished it and tried it on.

The Blusher Veil

Also called a "facial veil" or "Madonna veil," it is very short, only long enough to cover the face. It is often combined with a longer veil. You don't need a pattern for a blusher veil; just cut a piece of Illusion or tulle fabric 40 inches in diameter and shorten to the desired length.

The Waltz Veil

This is longer than a blusher veil, but shorter than a fingertip length. It is also called a "ballerina veil" or "elbow veil" because it ends at the bride's elbow. Use the pattern on page 67 and the instructions given on page 66, cutting from 108-inch-wide Illusion fabric.

The Fingertip Veil

This is a very popular length in the nineties; it hangs to the tips of the bride's fingers. Use the pattern and instructions given on the next two pages, cutting from 108-inch-wide Illusion fabric.

The Chapel Veil

This veil hangs to the floor and is worn with a floor-length wedding gown. Be sure to cut the fabric for this veil several inches longer than you want because it is important for it to touch the floor. Use the pattern and instructions given on the next two pages, cutting out of Illusion fabric 108 or 144 inches wide, depending on which width is most flattering with your gown.

The Cathedral Veil

This is the longest of the veils, extending at least 1 foot onto the floor, but it may extend as long as you like. A cathedral-length veil is very expensive to purchase retail, yet so affordable to make yourself. Use the pattern on page 67 and the instructions given below, cutting from Illusion fabric 144 inches wide. You need this width in order to have enough fullness at the end of your train.

The Mantilla Veil

The mantilla is made entirely of lace or Illusion nylon veil fabric trimmed with a wide lace edging. This is an extremely simple veil to make; you don't even need a pattern. Just cut a big circle in one of the following dimensions:

- Elbow length—36 inches in diameter
- Fingertip length—48 inches in diameter
- Chapel length—90 inches in diameter
- Cathedral length—108 inches in diameter

The mantilla is worn like a loose scarf, just framing the face. It is attached at the crown to a small hair comb; no frame is used.

Veils Attached to Hats

A small hat looks best with a short blusher veil. For a wide picture hat, wrap a folded length of Illusion or tulle fabric (36" × 108") around the brim. Tie it in a bow in the back and let it stream down the back of the gown. You can use this same fabric to attach under the back brim of a derby hat, also streaming down the back. There is no "right" or "wrong" about veiling a bridal hat; experiment until you like the way it looks with your gown. You can also add flowers, ribbons, pearls, sequins or lace.

It is not necessary to finish or trim the edges of Illusion or tulle veils because they will not ravel, but you may prefer to add lace trim.

Assembling the Veil

Following the pattern on page 67, gather the veil on the dotted lines. Leave 13 inches ungathered on each side. Using white carpet thread or unwaxed dental floss and a large-eyed needle, attach the gathered edge to your comb, hat, band, crown, silk flowers, bow or covered frame.

The Bride's Accessories

THE BRIDE'S SHOES

Purchase the most comfortable, yet affordable, white satin ballerina slippers, flats or pumps you can find and then decorate them yourself. (By the way, when you go shopping for shoes, be sure to buy a pair that's at least a half size larger than you normally wear because your feet will swell on your wedding day due to stress and being on your feet.) Here are a few inexpensive notions you can buy that will turn your bargain pair into exquisite bridal shoes. Visit your local craft or fabric store, grab your hot glue gun and have fun!

"Jewels"

Your craft store sells little sacks of sparkly embellishments, including tiny seed pearls, rhinestones and sequins. Or you can purchase a pair of "jeweled" clip-back earrings, remove

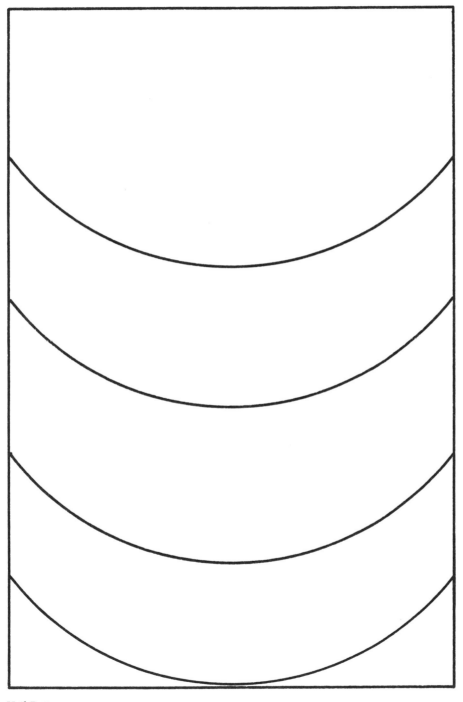

Veil Pattern

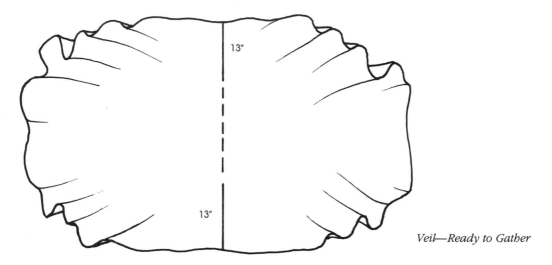

Veil—Ready to Gather

the clips and hot-glue one earring on each shoe. Another idea is to glue down matching strands of pearls, outlining the top of the shoe. You can also cover the heels of your shoes with "jewels" by gluing them one by one with the help of a pair of tweezers.

Bows

Purchase a pair of fancy hair bows (one bow per shoe, of course) or make your own out of satin, brocade, taffeta, moire, tulle netting, velvet, etc.

Lace Appliques

You can purchase elegant lace appliques, already cut and ready to use.

Silk Flowers

Wedding supply stores have walls full of wedding flower accessories with the stems beautifully wrapped and pearls or sequins already added.

Here is your chance to show your creativity! Why not combine some of these ideas? Glue tiny seed pearls to the bows? Add tufts of tulle netting under the silk flowers? Glue rhinestones or sequins to the appliqued lace? Everyone will think you special-ordered from Paris!

THE BRIDE'S GARTER

Enclose a piece of ½-inch elastic (about 15 or 16 inches long, so it fits comfortably above the knee) in blue satin fabric. Trim with white ruffled lace, ½ to 1½ inches wide. (You can also purchase ready-to-use "hoop lace.") Add a narrow satin acetate ribbon plus a tiny satin rosette, double white pearl hearts or other decorative novelty. You'll probably want to make two garters: one to toss at the reception and one to keep as a treasured memento.

THE BRIDE'S PURSE

It is a tradition in various cultures for a bride to wear a drawstring purse made out of white satin or lace. This custom goes back to the days when villagers would donate to the bride's dowry by dropping coins into her bridal purse.

You can make one of these purses out of a half yard of 54-inch-wide white satin or lace fabric. Fold the fabric so the right sides are together (the folded piece should now measure 18 inches high by approximately 27 inches wide). Stitch the top and bottom together, leaving the 18-inch side seam open. Turn the fabric right side out. Fold this piece in half (the folded piece should now measure 18 inches high by approximately 13½ inches wide). Sew the folded piece together at the bottom and side, leaving an opening at the top (approximately 13 inches wide). *Optional:* Add ruffled lace trim to the top of the opening of the purse.

To form casing for the drawstring, stitch around the top of the purse twice, placing the rows of stitches about ¾ inch apart. Start the first row of stitches about 3 inches down from the opening. After the rows are finished, with a small pair of sharp sewing scissors, cut two openings in the casing, one on each side of the purse. Using a safety pin, thread white cording through the casings on each side of the purse; pull the cording so it extends equally on each side; then cut and knot.

BRIDAL TRAIN RING

Many bridal gowns can be bustled by hooking the train at the back waistline for the reception. Another option, however, is the bridal train ring, a loop that holds the train of the gown enabling the bride to walk or dance during the reception without tripping.

This train ring is very easy to make: Simply cover a 10-inch embroidery hoop with a casing of white satin trimmed with 2-inch white lace, or use finished hoop lace. At the top of the ring add a white silk flower, narrow white satin acetate bows, and three 4-inch strands of tiny seed pearls.

The Bridal Bouquet

The classic bridal bouquet is a cluster of fresh flowers, fillers and greens, either hand-tied or inserted into a watered oasis inside a plastic bouquet holder. If ordered from a professional, full-service florist, here are the factors that will determine the bouquet's cost:

- The ratio of flowers to fillers and greens (the more flowers, of course, the more expensive the bouquet)
- Whether the flowers are "in season" or "out-of-season," hot house grown or natural, "pricey" or not
- Whether the flowers are individually wired and arranged, or placed in a "bunch" as a random arrangement
- The size of the bouquet (height by width)

Bridal Train Ring and Purse

Although there are several less expensive alternatives to the classic bridal bouquet (that I will mention in a moment), let's assume you are determined to have a full-sized, traditional, fresh flower bridal bouquet. If you have a talented do-it-yourself florist among your friends or family, your favorite bouquet can be duplicated for about 20 percent of its retail cost.

To select your favorite bouquet, search through bridal magazines and florists' catalogs. If you want a classic all-white bouquet, here are some of your floral choices:

- Camellias
- Easter lilies
- Gardenias
- Lilacs
- Stephanotis and hyacinths (mixed)
- Ranunculus
- Roses
- Stock and peonies mixed
- Queen Anne's lace
- Lily of the valley
- Astrantia and freesia (mixed)

If you're mixing colors into your bouquet, here are some floral suggestions, by season:

Spring

Tulips, lilacs, pansies, columbines, verbena, orange mint, poppies, geraniums, lilies of the valley, yarrow, muscari, tea roses, hydrangeas, daffodils, Iceland poppies, mimosa, peonies, violets.

Summer

Casablanca lilies, spray roses, wildflowers (sunflowers, zinnias, astilbes, hydrangeas, phlox, monarda, larkspur, blue lace, gooseneck veronica), miniature carnations, bachelor's buttons, bells of Ireland, clematis, delphinium, rosemary, sweet william.

Fall

Dahlias, puff hydrangea, sheaves of fresh wheat, classic roses, various orchids, bouvardia, China asters, chrysanthemums, statice, yarrow.

Winter

Cattleya orchids, sweet peas, cymbidium orchids, florabunda spray roses, stock, holly, red amaryllis, daffodils, hyacinths, paper whites, narcissus, heather, poinsettias, cyclamen, helleborus.

TRADITIONAL FRESH FLOWER BOUQUET

Once you've selected your bouquet's style and composition, order your flowers and filler greens from a wholesale fresh flower mart, to be picked up the day before the wedding, or use fresh flowers from your garden. Condition the flowers well to avoid the embarrassment of wilted blooms on the day of the wedding. To do this, cut the stems at an angle with a sharp knife *under water*. Add a commercial conditioner to the water, which will fill the stems with water until they become "hardened." Leave the flower stems under water for at least eight hours before arranging. With proper hardening, the flowers will retain enough water and stamina to last through the wedding day. Keep the flowers misted and cool until you are ready to build your bouquet.

Purchase these supplies ahead of time from your wedding or floral supply store:
- White plastic bouquet holder with floral foam
- One 10-inch, lace-edged form for bouquet holder
- 4 yards of no. 3 ribbon for a bow
- Narrow satin ribbon for "streamers"
- White florist tape
- Green florist tape
- No. 24- or no. 26-gauge floral wire

Depending on the style bouquet you have chosen, you will also need:
- Six to twenty-four stems of roses or flowers of your choice

- Five sprays of small-leafed ivy (for a cascade bouquet)
- Baby's breath
- Stephanotis
- Dried white gypsophila
- Lilies of the valley, bells of Ireland or others from the floral selection listed above, as required for the bouquet of your choice
- Holly or sprigs of evergreens (if a Christmas bouquet)

Set a photo or magazine picture of the bouquet you're going to copy in front of you as you work. Attach each individual flower to a strand of wire wrapped with green florist tape to simulate a stem, or actually thread a piece of wire up through the calyx and into the center of the flower. Some heavy flowers, such as roses or gladiolus, may need two wires. Cover any exposed wires with floral tape. Once all the flowers are wired, you are ready to manipulate them into the design you have chosen. Note: It is very important that the plastic bouquet holder be wrapped with ribbon or concealed with flowers or greenery. If it isn't, it may look "amateurish." (Although professional florists often use them bare without shame.)

General instructions for making a bridal bouquet using a bouquet holder:

- Wet the floral foam thoroughly using a mixture of half water and half 7-Up, plus one drop of household bleach.
- Attach the lace collar by pushing the handle of the bouquet holder through the center of the collar.
- Wrap the bouquet holder handle with ribbon or strips of fabric; tape securely at the top of the handle (where it meets the lace collar).
- Secure the lace collar with floral tape.
- Tie your ribbon(s) into a bow (leaving trailing ends if you wish); secure with a piece of wire, leaving a 4-inch twisted "stem." Set aside.
- Place all filler greenery securely in the floral foam (the trailing ivy or holly, etc.).
- Place the largest flowers in the floral foam, spacing according to the particular bouquet you are copying.
- Fill in the remaining spaces with the smaller flowers and filler flowers (such as baby's breath).
- Insert the stem of the bow and any hanging ribbons into the floral foam.
- When the bouquet is finished, mist it, cover it with plastic and refrigerate it until the very last minute. (Bring it to the ceremony site in an ice chest.)

SILK FLOWER BOUQUET

Create the same bouquet described above, only use silk flowers and greenery instead. There are several advantages to this alternative: Silk flower bouquets are less expensive, can be made ahead, and can be kept as mementos without preservation.

TUSSIE MUSSIE BOUQUET

This bouquet is created simply from fresh or dried flowers; it is less expensive and time-consuming than either of the first two options. Hand-tie the flowers together, with stems cut to a uniform length; insert the stems into a silver, cone-shaped tussie-mussie holder, which can be purchased at a wedding supply store or through a catalog.

POMANDER BOUQUET

The pomander (also known as a "globe") is a round ball covered with flowers, worn suspended by a ribbon that is looped over the bride's wrist. You may use fresh flowers inserted into a round water-saturated oasis, or silk flowers inserted into a Styrofoam ball. Before inserting the flowers into the ball, wrap a length of lace or ribbon (approximately 1 yard long) around the ball, leaving a 10-inch wrist loop at the top. Tie the ribbon in a knot at the bottom. Glue and pin the ribbon securely to the ball, leaving the wrist loop free at the top. Now you are ready to insert the flowers, covering the ball completely so that none of it is exposed. *Optional:* Use long florist pins or wood picks to tuck loops of ribbon or lace among the flowers.

HAND-TIED ARM BOUQUET

This is probably the easiest, most foolproof idea of all: Take a spray of fresh flowers, tie them at the stems with wide ribbon or lace. *Optional:* Cut off any excess leaves and stalks for a rich look of "blooms only."

HAND-TIED NOSEGAY

This is the same idea as the arm bouquet, only much smaller. Use six to eight small blooms and leave only about 6 inches of stalk, cut uniformly and tie with one or two simple bows, tails trailing down.

FABRIC-COVERED HAND BOUQUET

Similar to the nosegay, but larger, the hand bouquet usually includes about a dozen flowers. The stalks are left longer (about 10 inches from blooms to the ends of their stalks), then covered with fabric that matches the bride's gown. The fabric can be wrapped around the stalks in strips, or you can actually sew a "tube" of fabric to encase the stalks. *Optional:* Add bows at the top of the "tube" and let the tails trail down.

DECORATED BIBLE OR PRAYER BOOK

A white Bible or prayer book may be decorated with flowers, ribbons and lace, or it may be covered in white satin and then decorated. This is a very affordable idea, especially if you only use one flower, such as a large white orchid.

WHITE FAN DECORATED WITH FLOWERS

Purchase a ready-made lace fan or a plain bamboo and paper fan that can be covered with white satin and lace. Either of these fans can be embellished with a single flower, such as an orchid, or with a nosegay, plus a bow and trailing ribbons. *Optional:* Glue white pearl beads randomly over the top of the fan.

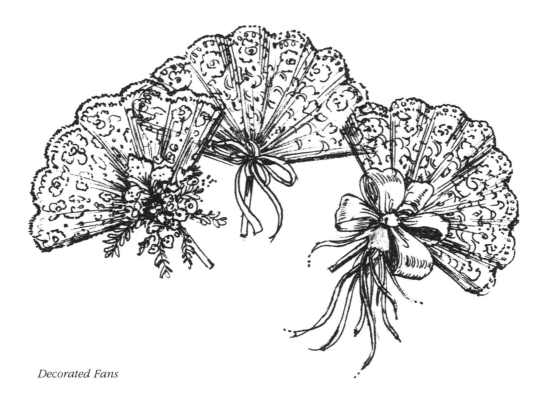

Decorated Fans

Bridal Attendants' Headpieces

SINGLE FLOWER OR BOW

A fresh or silk flower or single bow can be pinned onto the back or side of the head; be sure any flower stems are hidden under the hair. You may want to add narrow ribbons to the flower that trail to any length you like; if the tails hang longer than shoulder length, knot them about 6 inches from the end of each tail for style and stability. *Optional:* Add a tuft of tulle netting (6 to 10 inches long) gathered into the base of the flower or bow, or a longer strip of netting that floats along the floor.

DECORATED COMBS OR CLIPS

Have fun decorating ordinary hair combs or clips. Go to your craft or wedding supply store and purchase a few "jewels" or wedding novelty accessories; glue them to the combs or clips. A "banana clip" works especially well because you can decorate both sides of the clip.

DECORATED HATS

Whether you're decorating a pillbox, derby or picture hat, here is your chance to unleash your artistic talents. How about creating a "one-of-a-kind-gets-oohs-and-aahs-fun-to-photograph" hat for your bridesmaids? It's fine for their hats to be "overstated," as opposed to the more conservative style of a bridal hat. Once you have selected a style of hat that complements their dresses, start decorating to suit your wedding's theme. If your theme is Country, for example, how about a wide-brimmed hat rolled back at the forehead with a huge silk flower and a gingham ribbon bow? Or if your theme is more sophisticated, such as a Black and White wedding, add a tight blush veil of white tulle netting to a simple black pillbox (just enough to cover the face down to the bottom of the chin, also known as a birdcage veil). Or you might want to completely cover a picture hat in the same fabric as the bridesmaids' gowns or in swirls of tulle netting. Of course, traditional flowers (fresh or silk), wide ribbons, bows and trailing tulle netting are always fun to arrange on any wide-brimmed straw hat. Remember, you can spray paint a straw hat to complement the bridesmaids' dresses.

WREATH OF FRESH OR SILK FLOWERS

Use white or colored floral tape to help twist silk or fresh flowers into a hair wreath. Pin to the hair with bobby pins. *Optional:* Add narrow ribbons, tied into bows or trailing down in back.

Bridal Attendants' Accessories

SHOES

Flat ballet or toe shoes are being worn by more bridal attendants these days, the toe shoes usually with ankle-length dresses. Inexpensive satin pumps, already "dyed-to-match," may be ordered through Payless Shoes or another shoe outlet. Simply take a swatch of fabric to their store and compare it with the color chart (outdoors in strong sunlight, if possible) and place your order; the shoes arrive in about two weeks. These pumps can be embellished, if you like, with the same decorative notions as already suggested for the bride. An alternative to dyed-to-match shoes is white, gray, silver or gold.

PARASOL

Lace parasols come ready-made in various sizes, quite reasonably priced at wedding supply stores (about ten dollars for a medium-sized parasol). Or, you can purchase bamboo umbrellas from oriental import outlets; these can be used as is or spray painted in the color of your choice. Add flowers, ribbons, lace, seed pearls or bows of tulle netting.

Decorated Hat, Parasol and Shoes

Bridal Attendants' Flowers

All of the bridal bouquet ideas will also work for the bridal attendants, except, of course, the decorated Bible or prayer book. Follow the general directions for preserving the flowers and making the bouquets.

Here are a few floral ideas especially suited for the attendants:

BASKETS

Purchase deep or shallow white baskets from your wedding supply store, or buy plain brown wicker from your oriental import outlet. These baskets should be considerably larger than those usually carried by a flower girl. The brown wicker baskets can be spray painted any color you like, or covered completely in fabric the same as that of the bridesmaids' dresses. Fill the baskets with fresh or silk flowers (if fresh, anchor in water-filled oasis), and then add fabric ribbons and other novelty decorations suitable to your theme.

FLOWERS WRAPPED IN LACE OR DOILIES

Tie a simple bunch of flowers with floral tape, then fold wide antique lace or large white paper doilies around the stems. Poke a hole in the center of each doily so the stems will easily slide through. Add dainty bows at the base of the doilies or lace, plus trailing, knotted, narrow satin ribbons. This bouquet is especially suitable with a Country or Victorian wedding theme.

ROUND OR HEART-SHAPED WREATH

Decorate grapevine wreaths with flowers, lace, bows and trailing ribbons. Tie a 10-inch loop of fabric or satin acetate ribbon at the top of the wreath to be slipped over the bridesmaid's wrist. This bouquet complements a wreath wedding theme.

DECORATED CANDY CANES

Is it a Christmas wedding? Have fun decorating giant candy canes (straight or curved neck). Tie them with holly, mistletoe, sprigs of evergreens, silk stephanotis, white gypsophila, plus ribbon embellished with "gold dust" or "white snow" sparkles. *Optional:* Add one "showy" flower, such as a large white orchid or red poinsettia.

MUFF

Here is another cute idea for any winter wedding, including Christmas. Make a white fur muff out of rabbit's fur or fake fur fabric. Cut a piece 15 inches wide by 30 inches long; fold the piece in half with right sides together. (You will now have a piece 15 inches square.) Starting at the fold, stitch down each side, leaving the end open. Turn the right side out; then fold and stitch the open end to the finished end and turn the muff so this seam is on the inside. You now have a finished muff that can be decorated with a miniature nosegay and tiny ribbon bow with trailing ends, or with a single flower with dried white gypsophila.

SHEAVES OF WHEAT

Sheaves of wheat tied with single ribbons add pure and simple beauty to your wedding party. Gather a "bouquet" of wheat, cut the ends off uniformly, and tie with a single fabric ribbon. This bouquet is perfect for a Country wedding theme, and you sure can't complain about the cost!

SINGLE CANDLE IN BED OF FLOWERS

A single candle holder surrounded by a floral oasis or Styrofoam wreath is all you need as a foundation for this elegant bridesmaids' bouquet. Add a candle in your wedding color along with fresh or silk flowers, stephanotis, trailing ivy, and loops of ribbon or lace. This works nicely for a Candles, Candles, Candles theme; let the candles burn as the bridesmaids hold them throughout the ceremony.

Flower Girl's Accessories

BASKET

Purchase an inexpensive basket from your Oriental import shop or find one at a garage sale or around your house; spray paint it white or any color of your choice. A traditional Easter basket works well. If you're filling the basket with fresh flowers, place a water-filled oasis in the bottom. If filling the basket with silk flowers, you can use a Styrofoam base. Use small, delicate blooms with a touch of stephanotis; add a few strands of live or silk ivy (small leaf variety). Tie a bow to the handle of the basket.

If you're filling the basket with rose petals, add flowers, ribbon and lace to the front where the handle meets the basket itself.

HORSESHOE GARLAND

Here is one of the cutest ideas you've ever seen! Create a garland of flowers, or greenery with flowers added. You'll make the garland in the same way described earlier in this chapter, except you will need to wire everything to a rope running down the center of the garland. Any rope will work, but I prefer an ordinary cotton clothesline rope because I like to use a long carpet needle to sew loops of ribbon securely into the garland as I go. Tie the ends of the rope to create sturdy handles at each end.

Trim off the tail ends of the knots and wrap the handles with 2¾-inch satin acetate ribbon; be sure to cover the rope handles completely. Add 3-yard satin acetate bows at each end of the garland, or use moire or taffeta ribbon instead. Depending on the theme of your wedding, you may want to make bows out of wide strips of fabric, such as checked gingham or red velvet. The garland can be anywhere from 3 feet long (to be held by one girl with one handle in each hand) to 8 feet long (which requires two flower girls, one on each side of the horseshoe). When the flower girl(s) reach the altar, the garland may be placed on it or beneath it as part of the ceremony decorations, or the girl(s) may hold the horseshoe garland throughout the ceremony. If two flower girls are involved, be sure they practice walking down the aisle in unison; the whole effect is lost if one is walking ahead of the other. And tell them to walk *slowly* because they will be a precious prelude to the wedding march and the enchanting sight should be savored!

FLORAL NECKLACE

Connect floral blooms together into a necklace, using white unwaxed dental floss and a large-eyed needle. Tie the ends together after the necklace is in place and trim any excess dental floss close enough to be out of sight, but not so short that the necklace comes untied.

DECORATED SASH

If the flower girl's dress has a wide sash that ties in back, decorate the sash's bow with fresh or silk flowers. Sew the flowers in and among the folds of the bow *after* the bow has been tied; use heavy carpet thread the color of the sash. This creates an unusually interesting and cute "rear view" as she walks down the aisle.

HAIR DECORATIONS

Several ideas given for bridal attendants also work well for a flower girl, including a single flower or bow, decorated comb or hair clip, floral wreath or decorated hat. Everything should be in proportion to the size of the child, especially the hat. A small white straw hat with a

Rope for Floral Horseshoe

Floral Horseshoe

narrow rolled-up brim is easy to decorate by filling the brim with silk or fresh flowers. Pony tail wreaths can be created in the same way as the floral necklace, described above. Another sweet use of flowers is to pin several tiny rosebuds (no leaves or long stems) directly into the girl's back or side curls so they appear to be peeking out. You can also create a "tiara" of fresh or silk flowers by binding the flowers to a plastic headband using white floral tape.

PARASOL

Use the same instructions already given for the bridal attendant's parasol, except be sure the size of the parasol itself, plus any decorative flowers, ribbons, etc., are in proportion to the size of the girl.

Other accessories might be a smaller version of the bride's nosegay bouquet using narrower ribbon; a pomander made using the instructions already given and substituting a smaller "globe"; a single long-stemmed rose (if the girl is very small, make sure the rose isn't *too* long); or a mini arm bouquet that is a miniature reproduction of the bride's arm bouquet described earlier in this chapter.

Men's Boutonnieres

There are two general types of wedding boutonnieres: the "traditional" (single rose, sprig of stephanotis or lily of the valley) and the "lapel spray," a more elaborate boutonniere worn only by the groom. The lapel spray is larger and fancier than the others and may contain flowers and greenery from the bride's bouquet. A traditional boutonniere can be as simple as a single rose with a bare, unwrapped stem, to a flower and sprig of baby's breath on a single leaf background, all wrapped with floral tape and tied with a narrow ribbon. Be sure to wire the main flower to keep it from drooping during the ceremony. Any boutonniere is inexpensive and easy to make yourself. It is always worn on the man's left lapel. Any extra ushers, by the way, usually wear plain carnation boutonnieres.

Ring Bearer's Accessories

BOUTONNIERE

The ring bearer's boutonniere is made the same way as the "traditional" boutonniere described above, only in proportion to the boy's size.

PILLOW

Cut two pieces of white satin or moire fabric, each 11 inches by 13 inches, or two heart-shaped pieces approximately the same size. (Enlarge the heart pattern in chapter one.) Place the two pieces of fabric with right sides together and stitch around the outer edges, leaving a 3-inch opening at the top. Turn right-side-out, press flat, fill with loose polyester batting, and close the opening with hand stitching. Trim around the outside edge of the pillow by hand stitching ruffled lace 1 to 3 inches in width. Use your hot glue gun to tack on any delicate embellishments, such as tiny satin bows, twin-pearl hearts, silk rosette buds, strips of delicate flat lace, wedding appliques and "pretend" gold rings (unless you plan to give him the real thing). You can hand-stitch a 4-inch strip of ribbon onto the bottom of the pillow to help your ring bearer hold the pillow nice and flat. One precaution: Don't make the pillow without matching the whites; you don't want a "blue-white" pillow next to a cream or ivory wedding gown because it will make the gown look dirty.

Mothers' Flowers

CORSAGE

Before choosing a corsage for the mothers and grandmothers, take into consideration each woman's height and size, plus the style and color of her dress. Traditionally, mothers' corsages are composed of orchids or roses, but there are a variety of other choices. My mother's favorite flower, for example, is the gardenia, so this is obviously what she would prefer; also, she is quite petite, so we wouldn't want to weigh her down with an oversized corsage. A small one gardenia corsage would be fine.

The easiest way to make a mother's corsage, or any corsage for that matter, is to use ready-made corsage forms (also called "corsage backs"). They come with or without ribbon, but I suggest you add your own ribbon, which will be fuller and prettier than those that come on the ready-mades. These corsage forms, by the way, can be purchased at any floral or wedding supply store. They are already wrapped and embellished; all they need are your fresh or silk flowers and greenery. Again, be sure to wire any fresh flowers so the corsage will hold its shape through the ceremony.

Buy a couple of the corsage forms ahead of time and practice by wiring and inserting fresh flowers from your garden; you'll gain instant confidence and probably never purchase corsages from a retail florist again.

WRISTLET

Wristlet is just another word for "wrist corsage." With some of today's delicate fabrics, there is no way to pin a regular corsage on a dress without damaging it, so just convert the corsage into a "wristlet" by adding a ready-to-use elastic wristband, also available at your floral or wedding supply store.

SINGLE LONG-STEMMED ROSE

Each mother can carry a single long-stemmed rose, with or without a single ribbon tied to its stem. Sometimes the bride carries two of these roses with her down the aisle, gives one to her mother after her father "gives her away" and the other to her new mother-in-law before the recessional.

5

The Reception

*T*he ceremony is over, and all went well! Now, it's time to smile and have some fun at the reception. A wedding reception is probably one of the biggest parties a family will ever give, and you want it to be great—only not too expensive, right? So, how do we throw this great party on a budget? By doing the "crafting" and "creating" ourselves. This chapter offers several dozen easy, affordable ideas to create that special ambiance for your party.

Themes

Here we are, back to the question of themes again, because the theme not only makes the planning easier, but creates the ambiance for your reception. With the right theme, you can put your guests into another time or another world, one they're reluctant to leave when the party's over!

First of all, look back through chapter four and you will notice that most of the themes suggested there can be carried right through to the reception. Also, chapter one has several engagement party themes that can also be used for a reception, only on a larger scale, such as the Spring Garden Party, Country-Western, Nostalgia, Polynesian and the Fifties Sock Hop. Here are more themes for you to consider:

- Hearts and Flowers
- Rose Garden
- Summer in the Park
- Paris in Springtime
- Cupids and Hearts
- Victorian Tea Party
- Ice Palace
- Winter Wonderland
- Romantic Candlelight
- Autumn Harvest
- Christmas Joy
- Valentine's
- *Gone With the Wind*
- Gay Nineties
- Roaring Twenties
- Renaissance Festival
- Tropical Rain Forest
- Carousel
- Mississippi Riverboat
- The *Love Boat*
- A Hollywood Movie Set
- Mountain Ski Resort

Ethnic Themes:

- Mexican Fiesta
- Chinatown
- "When Irish Eyes Are Smiling"
- Scandinavian Love Feast
- Canadian Sunset
- African Safari
- German or Austrian Oktoberfest
- Love in the Alps

Customized Themes:

Or, how about customizing the theme to the couple's vocations, hobbies or interests? For example, if the groom is an airline pilot, create an "airport" theme, complete with a "runway" for the receiving line, a cake top made out of a toy airplane sitting on a "cloud" of tulle netting, with the couple's names painted on the side, and a "Just Married" banner flying off the tail of the plane. Miniature copies of this little airplane can be given as favors.

Another couple may be into hot air ballooning. How about having them stand inside an actual basket during the receiving line, or having a cake top made from a miniature hot air balloon, also with their names and a "Just Married" banner, and maybe they can even use a hot air balloon as their "getaway" vehicle.

Then there's the groom who loves to race cars—he's out at the stock car races every Saturday night. Why not turn the reception hall into an Indy 500 race track? Have an actual, full-sized race car in the hall or on the site? Hang victory wreaths of flowers around the couple's necks? Give them a pint of milk to drink? Decorate with racing flags? Make a cake top out of a mini race car, again with the names and banner and maybe a checkered flag?

The key is to let your imagination run free! See how it works? Avoid the typical reception with the "cookie-cutter" look! Dare to be original.

Basic Props

As you consider the possibility of a personalized, customized theme for the bride and groom, here are some of the basic "props" that can be used to create some of these theme illusions:

BALLOONS

Whether you only use a "bouquet" of balloons here and there around your reception hall, or you use hundreds of balloons as the main attraction at your party, they are an economical way to decorate. They splash a lot of color for the money and are a clever substitute for flowers. Here are some good ways to use balloons:

Archways

Helium balloons, when attached to a fishing line held down at each end with heavy bricks, will form a natural arch. With no help at all, a line full of helium balloons will *insist* on arching at the center! (How convenient!) So, use this wonderful law of physics to your advantage by making balloon arches over the head table, the cake table, from end to end of the receiving line, or for the guests to walk under as they enter the reception hall.

Backs of Chairs

Tie a helium balloon on the back of each chair. The trick is to have the balloons at different heights so the cross-view of the room shows a lot of color.

Frame Doorways and Windows

You can use helium balloons, but air-filled balloons work just as well. Fill the sides of all the doorways and windows with individual balloons close together. You can fill in between the balloons if you'd like with crinkle tie ribbon clusters or silk flowers.

Cover the Ceiling

Attach one helium balloon to one regular balloon; tie them with crinkle tie ribbon at their nipples. Leave some curled ribbon hanging down, then release them and they will float to the ceiling. Or, you can use only helium balloons with long ribbons attached, release them to the ceiling during the reception, then have each guest "catch" one to take outside and release into the sky as the couple drives off in their getaway vehicle.

Table Centerpieces

You can use helium balloons as "bouquets" growing out of vases on the tables, or you can inflate regular balloons and tie them to a fishing line that extends along the center of the table. Add clusters of ribbons and a few silk flowers or greenery among the balloons. Another centerpiece idea is to cluster three helium balloons and thread their ribbon tails inside a tissue wedding bell. The trick is to keep the bell from floating up with the balloons; you can do this by attaching a heavy metal bolt, washer or chrome ring to the ribbon tails and enclosing them inside the tissue bell.

A Flower Garden

If your theme calls for a garden, use white picket fencing to outline your garden of balloon "flowers." Use tape to attach the ribbon streamers to the floor. Have your "flowers" growing at varying heights. You can add potted trees or plants as a background for your garden.

Cover Mantles and Bannisters

Make "garlands" of balloons by stringing them along fishing line to cover mantles, bannisters, and any other bare spots in the room.

Cover Wire Frames

If you really want to get fancy, make frames out of wood or wire and outline them with balloons. A popular shape at a wedding reception, of course, is a large heart.

Create Columns

Use either helium or regular balloons to give the illusion of vertical columns throughout the room. You can suspend a wire, white plastic clothesline or fishing line from ceiling to floor, then tape the nipples of the balloons as close together as possible.

Balloon Drop

Fill the balloons with air instead of helium and suspend them from the ceiling in nets. At a designated time during the reception, release the nets so the balloons will float down over the guests.

If you're going to create balloon decorations yourself, as opposed to paying retail price through a florist, you might as well do it right, so buy good quality latex balloons, whether using helium or not. You can do your balloon decorating the day before the wedding by using a product called Hi-Float, which coats the inside of the balloon to prevent helium from escaping through the latex. A helium balloon without this product will only float for about eighteen hours, but with it for three to five days! By the way, if you use foil or Mylar balloons, you won't need to worry about this because they will last for weeks without Hi-Float.

Purchase your balloons and Hi-Float, along with disposable or rented helium tanks, at a balloon wholesale supply house. Look in your yellow pages under "balloons." If your area isn't large enough to have one of these specialty outlets, purchase your supplies from a wedding supply or party shop.

TULLE NETTING OR CHIFFON FABRIC

Here is another way to decorate effectively with very little expense. In the last chapter we learned some clever ways to use tulle netting: swagging, draping, swirling, twirling and tying into bows. Well, it can do even more for your reception hall because you can buy it by the bolt and swag it across the front of all your tables, tying it up in bows every 3 feet; swirl it over and around gazebos, trellises and latticework; or drape it over windows and doorways.

Tulle netting or any chiffon-like white fabric also can be used to create something literally out of thin air. Full, puffy columns of netting or fabric can be created by suspending heavy cord or white plastic clothesline from ceiling to floor. Gather the netting or fabric around the suspended line, starting at the ceiling and cinching in at its "waistline" every 2 or 3 feet by tying it tightly to the line with ribbon.

An entire gazebo can be created out of the gauzy fabric by using the columns we just described as the corners and forming a "roof" out of a 20-foot-square piece of the fabric. (Sew together four widths of 60-inch fabric by about 7 yards long.) Thread a heavy fishing line through a 6-inch section at the center of this square piece and draw the fabric up to the ceiling, creating a pointed roof. Then bring the corners of the fabric over to meet the four columns; tie them into the vertical lines supporting the columns.

You'll be surprised what a little netting and fabric can do to set the mood for your theme.

CANDLES AND LIGHTS

Candles and strings of small white Christmas tree lights can do wonders, as well. In fact, if you've been to any high school proms lately, you've probably discovered that the two decorating props they use most often are balloons and white Christmas tree lights. You see, they are forced to convert a huge, ugly gym into an "awesomely romantic" ballroom, and what better way than by using these inexpensive props.

If your reception is being held in a rather unexciting spot, schedule it in the evening so you can set the mood with lighting. First of all, if you don't want your guests to notice the unglamorous setting, keep the regular lights low and substitute as many candles as you can

Fabric Column

Fabric Gazebo

afford, along with strings of little white lights. Fill in around the edges with borrowed plants or potted trees; then "twinkle them up" with the lights. Swirl the lights around the cake table, over doorways and trellises—everywhere you can to give the room a "wonderland" setting.

GARLANDS

You remember these from chapter four! They work just as well, if not better, to decorate a reception site. Swag them around the fronts of the serving tables and cake table and drape them over doorways and window frames.

POTTED FLOWERS AND SILK TREES

Raid the homes and patios of your closest friends and relatives to gather up a supply of flowers and trees. Space them around the room or use them to divide spaces within the room, which will create a more intimate, cozy feeling.

If you decide to purchase a few flowering plants, buy them from a local discount nursery; wrap the containers in cellophane or foil paper and tie them with bows. Or, you usually can find them already wrapped and on sale through your supermarket florist. Either way, you'll save about 75 percent off the price through a full-service retail florist.

SPECIALITY PROPS

In addition to the general ideas I have given above, you will need certain speciality props. Once you have decided on your theme, you will come up with a list of things you need, many of which may seem impossible to find. However, think of it as a merry scavenger hunt (remember how much fun they were?) and go out there and beg, borrow and steal! Here are just a few things that are bought, borrowed or rented for wedding receptions:

Canopy	Gazebo
Dance floor	Mirror ball
Antique street lamps	Park benches
Bird baths	Fountains
Waterfalls	Trellises
Latticework	Arbors
Picket fences	Carousel horses
Antique popcorn machines	Wishing well
Patio furniture	Portable "bridges"
Globe lamps	Pagodas
Wading pools with live ducks	Baskets
Tiki torches	Huge paper flowers
Screens	Tissue paper bells
Rafts (for the pool)	Parasols
Crepe paper streamers	Potted ferns
Tents	Decorated fans
Oriental lanterns	Pinwheels
Grape vines	Tubs of pansies, etc.
Wind chimes	Serapes
Old family wedding photos	Piñatas
Bird cages (with or without the birds)	

Note: Re-use as many ceremony decorations as possible by "hustling" them to the reception site immediately after the guests have been ushered out.

Table Decorations

Unless you have a full dinner or luncheon buffet or a sit-down meal, you may not need formal table seating at your reception. Guests can usually manage plates of light finger foods while standing or sitting at individual chairs placed around the room. In this case, you will only need to worry about decorations for the buffet table. However, if your meal does require formal seating, there are several ways to arrange the tables. Probably the most popular is to have one long head table for the bridal party, plus individual tables for the rest of the guests. The traditional seating at the head table is for the bride and groom to sit in the center with the maid of honor next to the groom and the best man next to the bride. The rest of the bridesmaids and groomsmen alternate boy-girl-boy-girl for the remaining seating.

If there is no head table, you will need to have at least two regular tables reserved for the bridal party, parents, grandparents and clergy. Here is suggested seating for these two tables:

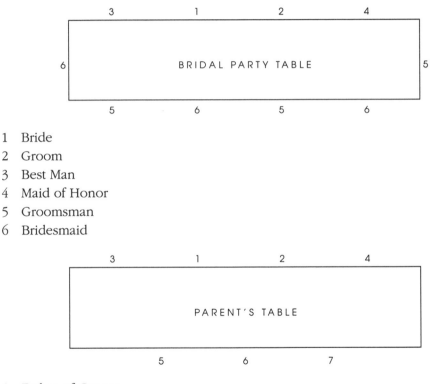

1 Bride
2 Groom
3 Best Man
4 Maid of Honor
5 Groomsman
6 Bridesmaid

1 Father of Groom
2 Mother of Bride
3 Grandmother
4 Clergy
5 Father of Bride
6 Mother of Groom
7 Grandfather

The Buffet Table

You know what great chefs always say: "It's all in the presentation!" And that's so true. You can make even the most ordinary food seem special with glamorous presentation!

Elevate the Food

Have you ever noticed that Sunday brunch at an expensive restaurant always looks so dramatic? Well, their first trick is that they elevate all the food dishes. You probably never even noticed that the dishes are "cascaded" down from the back to the front of the table. Build up levels by covering heavy books or cigar boxes weighted with bricks. You can use linen napkins or just place them under the tablecloth itself and work the cloth in and around your props. This will create interesting "mounds" and "valleys."

Fill in the "Valleys"

Add color and splash to the table by filling all those valleys with as much eye appeal as possible—flowers, greenery, ribbons, crepe paper, candles, large pieces of fresh fruit, bottles of champagne, etc.—just like they do at those Sunday brunchs! (Be sure to add a few theme novelties, such as doves, bells or hearts.)

Garnish Each Dish

In addition to tucking color in and around, you'll also need to garnish the individual food trays themselves. Use green leafy lettuce, parsley, huge strawberries, melon slices, pineapple chunks and fresh flowers.

Ice Sculpture Centerpiece

I know what you're saying, "Hey, these are supposed to be *affordable* ideas!" Well, this is *very* affordable because there's a way to "do-it-yourself." Go to your local wholesale food or catering supplier and purchase an ice sculpture mold. They range from about 1 to 3 feet high and cost from twenty to forty-five dollars. This is the only basic expense you'll have, other than the food coloring you might add to the water. There are many molds to choose from: hearts, swans, love doves, a bride and groom kissing, etc. Once you own one of these molds, you can re-use it again and again. You simply fill it with water (colored if you'd like) and freeze it solid. Unmold it by briefly dipping in a tub of warm water (the same way you unmold Jello). Place the ice sculpture on a bed of crushed ice scattered with fresh flowers. At our daughter's wedding we had a burgundy swan ice sculpture that sat in a big punch bowl full of crushed ice. As the swan slowly began to melt during the afternoon, the burgundy drizzles made an interesting design as they slithered down through the crushed ice. This centerpiece was such a hit (I don't think our little California valley town had ever seen anything like it!) that we actually had guests photographing the thing. Not only that, but they wanted to be *in* the photo with the swan. Can you believe it? All for the mere cost of a twenty-two-dollar mold!

THE HEAD TABLE

The head table decorations are usually a little more elaborate than for the other tables. Here are some suggestions:

Table "Dressing"

Dress up the head table by draping tulle netting or swags of moire or taffeta fabric along the front of the table, pulling it up every few feet and tying in a large tulle net or satin acetate ribbon. Be sure to skirt the table all the way to the floor. You can purchase inexpensive disposable table skirting or make your own by gathering tulle netting (triple the length of the table for enough fullness).

If you have a Christmas theme, wrap the head table up like a big gift. Run 4-inch ribbon down the center of the table so it overlaps the sides and tucks under the table skirting; run another piece of ribbon from back to front over the center of the table, also tucking under the table skirting. At the very center of the top of the table, tie an oversized bow, which will become the table's centerpiece.

Center Runner

Fill the entire length of the table with a center runner of tulle netting, balloons, evergreen garlands, bows, or line the center with mirror squares sprinkled with rose petals. *Optional:* Trail gently twisted narrow ribbon down the length of the table, on top of the evergreen garlands, or in and around the rose petals.

Flowers for the Head Table

Use the bridesmaids' bouquets as floral arrangements for the head table. Place them toward the outside of the table so they may be seen by the guests, with any ribbons trailing down over the front of the tablecloth. If you decide against using their bouquets on the head table, you can use any of the centerpiece suggestions given later in this chapter.

Dress Up the Place Settings

Whether you use fine china or paper plates, dress up your place settings. Tie bows around a piece of silverware or the stem of a champagne glass; fancy-fold the napkins; use elegant place cards. Chapter three has some of these good ideas, including these place cards, the first four of which can double as favors:

- Gold truffle boxes
- Personalized picture frames
- Personalized napkin rings
- Individual bud vases
- Wedding bell place cards

THE GUEST TABLES

The guest tables don't necessarily need skirting, although that is a nice added touch, and you don't need the swags of decorative netting or center runners, but you do want the place settings to be exquisite and inviting. Make your guests feel special by adding a ribbon, wreath or balloon to each chair, and use the same place setting ideas as for the head table. You will only need place cards, however, at the reserved tables. Each table will also need a distinctive centerpiece.

Table Centerpieces

These are some of the formal centerpieces that were already described in chapter three:

- Candles and mirrors
- Miniature topiaries
- Antique china arrangements
- Evergreens and dried herbs
- Candlesticks with floral wreaths
- Hurricane chimneys on mirrors
- Wine glasses on mirrors
- Cake pedestals with figurines

Here are a few more less formal ideas for you to consider:

- *Three Milk Glass Bud Vases*: Hit up all the garage sales and flea markets for varied sizes and heights of white milk glass vases; most have several for sale. Cluster them in groups of three in the center of each table, filling each vase with a single flower. Tie each vase at the neck with a ribbon.
- *Watermelon Vase*: This informal floral centerpiece is the perfect conversation piece for a casual picnic-style reception. Cut a small watermelon in half lengthwise and use the insides as an oasis for an arrangement of any "country" flowers, such as wildflowers or daisies.
- *Candle and Evergreen Wreath*: Surround a single candle with sprigs of evergreenery wired into a wreath. Add small red Christmas balls or ornaments depicting your theme; tie a coordinating ribbon around the candle. Tuck a little dried white gypsophila among the greenery.
- *Apple Candles and Autumn Leaves*: Round up some shallow wicker paper plate holders and set three red apples in the center, each with its stem and core removed. Insert 9-inch candles. Tie the candles with raffia and fill the rest of the plate holders with bright colored fall leaves. This centerpiece, of course, is perfect for an autumn wedding theme.

- *Grapevines and Candles:* Place a 12-inch grapevine wreath flat in the center of the table; add a candle inside a hurricane chimney and fill in between the grapevine and the chimney with fresh or silk ivy and stephanotis, letting the ivy "crawl" up onto the grapevine as it will.
- *"Blooming" Balloons:* Use any decorative pot or vase and "plant" a bouquet of small helium balloons, as suggested earlier in this chapter.
- *Flowers in Flowerpots:* Use a simple clay flowerpot as the base for flowering bulbs, such as tulips, daffodils or white crocus, or bedding plants, such as petunias, pansies or impatiens. Wrap the pot in cellophane or any fabric that complements your theme, such as white brocade, checked gingham or blue taffeta. Tie with a bow and set in a bed of colored Easter grass.
- *Flowering Hats:* Turn a black top hat, sombrero or straw hat upside down and "plant" it with a full bouquet of fresh flowers and greenery. Use a heavy coffee mug or jar for stability; fill it so full of flowers and greens that the container is hidden.

Mix and Match

Mix and match these ideas to create your own imaginative centerpiece relating to your theme:

Fans	Parasols
Pine cones	Tiny "pumpkin" gourds
Raffia	Strawflowers
Cactus gardens	Fruit
Pieces of artwork, such as sculpture	Small birdbaths
Fishbowls (including fish)	Figurines
Child's watering can (spray painted)	Small flags
Ethnic novelties (such as a Swedish horse or Dutch windmill)	Jewelry
	Magnolia, lilac or orange blossoms
Small stuffed animals or toys	Polished agates
Seashells	Dried herbs and grasses
Cattails	Bells
Antique lace	Christmas ornaments used as centerpiece
Red-foiled hearts	figures, such as a rocking horse

THE CAKE TABLE

The table itself should be a showpiece: it should be skirted, preferably with tulle netting, as well as the regular paper or plastic skirting, and decorated with flowers, garlands, ribbons, bows, swirls of tulle netting, balloons or the bridesmaids' bouquets (if they aren't already being used to decorate the head table). Add large net or ribbon bows on the front of the table, as well.

The Dummy Wedding Cake

This has been one of the most popular suggestions in my book, *How to Have a Big Wedding on a Small Budget*, so I feel obligated to include it for you here. A dummy wedding cake is simply a "fake" cake made out of Styrofoam layers (purchased at hobby or bakery supply stores). The layers come in 6-, 8- and 12-inch rounds; assemble them as high and wide as you like. The top layer should be the "real thing," however, so it can be frozen and served on the couple's first anniversary. Frost the cake with simple white butter cream frosting and then decorate the layers yourself, using fresh or silk flowers, winding ivy, ribbons or a cake top. Bake a real cake (about 4 inches round) that sits between the dummy cake and the bride and groom; this is what they cut. Or, you may cut a wedge out of the bottom Styrofoam layer and fill with the real thing for this purpose. Serve the guests from homemade sheet cakes out of the kitchen! (Believe it or not, the guests never figure this out!)

Cake Toppers

There are dozens of affordable cake toppers you can make yourself. Here are a few to choose from:

- *Fresh Flowers*: On the morning of the wedding, purchase fresh flowers from your supermarket florist or cut them from your own yard; place them on top of the cake, as well as on each layer. Or, you can "wrap" the cake on a diagonal with a garland of flowers. *Optional*: Add occasional checked gingham single bows.
- *Gift Wrap Topper*: Use 2¾-inch ribbon to "wrap" the cake like a gift—use four pieces of ribbon, each secured under one of the four sides of the bottom of the cake. Bring each piece all the way to the top of the cake; secure the ends with long plastic cocktail toothpicks. Make a 3-yard bow (see chapter two for directions). Place the bow on top of the cake with narrow trailing ribbons hanging down on all sides of the cake.
- *Heart With Hanging Love Doves*: Form a heart shape out of 18-gauge floral wire, thread the wire through the casing of ready-to-use ruffled hoop lace, and mount the bottom of the heart in a round piece of Styrofoam (about 4 inches wide by 1 inch high). Cover the Styrofoam with white ruffled lace approximately 3 inches wide; suspend two lightweight white satin doves from the top of the heart. (These doves can be purchased from a Christmas shop as tree ornaments for about $1.25 each.) Gently press the Styrofoam base onto the top of the cake; add tufts of white tulle netting on and around the Styrofoam base.
- *Wine Glass With Flowers*: Stand a wine glass on a round mirror for stability; fill with silk flowers and tufted netting. Tie the stem of the glass with a bow. Add swirls of netting around the outside of the mirror.
- *Photo of the Bride and Groom*: Frame a formal photo of the bride and groom in an elegant white ceramic or lacy frame; set it on a 5″ × 1″ base of white Styrofoam. Cover the base with silk flowers, tufts of tulle netting, and strings of white pearls. Drape a strand of the pearls over an upper corner of the frame.

- *Tiny White Basket With Flowers*: Find the most "precious" little basket possible, one with a handle. Spray it white and fill it with silk daisies. Tie the handle with checked gingham ribbon.

- *Ruffled Lace Tied With Flowers*: Purchase 2 yards of 8-inch-wide white drawstring lace; draw the string to ruffle the lace. The lace will be so full at the base that it will sit by itself on the top of the cake. Tie the lace (over the drawstring) with ribbon and a cluster of three silk flowers in the wedding colors.

- *Bride and Groom Figurines*: Set a ceramic or bisque bride and groom on a mirror on the top of the cake. Add dozens of sprigs of white stephanotis, not only around the feet of the couple, but scattered randomly down from layer to layer. (Insert the stems of the flowers into the sides of the cake, as well as onto the tops of each layer and around the base of the cake.)

- *Open Book*: Start with any small book, such as the "fit-in-the-palm" Golden Books for children. Fold the pages open at the center of the book; glue all the pages together on both sides of the center. (Use white craft glue applying a thin coat between each page, leaving the very edges of the pages free.) Once the pages have dried, spray paint the book with gold glitter spray paint. Cut two pages out of white linen paper; glue them down in the center of the book. Using a fineline glitter paint pen, write the couple's names on one page. Using liquid embroidery pens, make a floral design in the corner of the other page. On that same page, glue two small gold rings. Lay this little book on a full bed of curled ribbons, in your wedding colors or metallic gold to match the gold leaves of the book. Add a narrow ribbon in between the two center pages as a "bookmark." Glue the ribbon to the top of the book, but let it extend loosely below the book, the way ribbon bookmarks usually do. (See the illustration below.)

Double Rings and Open Book

- *Two Pearl Rings*: Start with a Styrofoam base approximately 4 inches in diameter, by about 1 inch thick. Glue a 3-inch Styrofoam ball to the center of this base. Form two "rings" out of 18-gauge floral wire, leaving about 1½ inches of wire extended to be used to secure the rings to the ball. Cover each ring with white satin fabric or ribbon, then cover the top with strings of pearls (which can be purchased as Pearls-by-the-Yard at crafts stores). Use your hot glue gun to attach these strings of pearls. Mount the rings into the ball, then add tufts of tulle netting and small white silk flowers at the base of the rings. Glue the same strings of pearls around the outside of six or eight white silk leaves; then add them as well by sticking their stems into the Styrofoam ball. Top it all off with a yard of 5-inch-wide white drawstring lace, drawn up tight at the base of the ball.

- *Double Hearts*: Use the same directions given above for the two pearl rings, only form the 18-gauge wire into heart shapes instead.
- *Gazebos or Arches*: Purchase unassembled gazebos or arches from your wedding supply store; assemble and fill with fresh or silk flowers, ivy and baby's breath.
- *Blown Glass*: There are many blown glass figures that work well as wedding cake toppers, including hanging pieces, such as bells, that can be suspended from a lace heart, as described above.
- *Music Box With Rotating Figure*: Here's an easy one! And will it ever be a hit. Borrow a music box that complements your theme; for example, love doves or a carousel horse. Set it on a circular mirror so it can be wound easily off and on during the reception. Surround the box with flowers, ribbon, ivy or tulle netting.
- *"Precious Moments" Bride and Groom*: Do you know anyone who collects Precious Moments figurines? If so, ask to borrow their bride and groom to use as a cake top. Place a 4- or 5-inch round mirror on top of the cake to be used as a base for the figurine. Then decorate around the edges of the mirror with tiny rosebuds and fern.
- *Airplane With Just Married Sign*: Purchase or assemble a miniature airplane. Write the couple's names on the side. Attach a "Just Married" sign with miniature flowers and streamers to the tail of the plane.
- *Toy Race Car With Just Married Sign*: Do the same with a toy race car; add a black and white checkered flag.
- *Customized Bride and Groom*: Purchase a ceramic or porcelain bride and groom that look as much as possible like the wedding couple; dress them up in replicas of their actual wedding attire, or outfits depicting their hobbies, vocations or interests or complementing the wedding theme (twenties flapper dress and coonskin hat, Victorian costumes, military uniform, fifties poodle skirt and jeans and white tee shirt, nineties saloon dress and gambler's suit, or a couple wearing cowboy hats "lassoed" inside a circle of rough rope tied with a double knot).
- *Teddy Bear Bride and Groom*: Dress up two tiny bears as bride and groom (see the opening page of this chapter). *Optional*: Have them stand in a miniature hot air balloon (with tiny helium balloon attached) or surrounded by tufts of tulle netting or under a heart (similar to the heart-shaped topper described above).
- *Customized Theme Topper*: Use a novelty item relating to your theme; place it in the

center of the top layer. Decorate around it with lace, flowers, greenery, ribbons, or whatever is appropriate. Examples: *Polynesian Theme*—Tiny ukulele and flower lei; *Christmas Theme*—Novelty ornaments, such as a rocking horse or sleigh; *Hollywood Theme*—Megaphone that says "Bob and Anna's Big Day"; *Mountain Ski Resort*—Two miniature pairs of skis, "plunged" into the frosting, as if into the snow; write the bride's and groom's names on the skis. Paint popsicle or craft sticks in the wedding colors and tie with narrow strands of suede lace, which will serve as "bindings." Packages of suede lace are available at craft stores.

- *Copy Your Favorite Topper.* This is easier than you may think, because wedding supply stores and many craft stores sell the component parts you will need to duplicate a cake topper you may have seen in a bakery, magazine, stationery store or bridal shop. My only word of caution is this: Be very careful that you don't end up spending more for the "parts" than the retail price for the "whole." Unless you shop carefully, you may spend more than you should to copy a topper. In one store, for example, I found Pearls-by-the-Yard on sale at four different prices, depending on where they were in the store. In their craft supply department, they were priced at $1.00 for 5 yards; in their fabric trim department, they were $2.99 a yard; in their bridal sewing supply corner, a similar product was $9.95 per yard. The same holds true for Styrofoam bases, hearts, balls, hoop lace, flat lace, drawstring lace, ribbon, silk flowers and leaves, and all the other novelties you may need to create a cake topper. So, make a list, shop around, compare prices, and then decide whether it is worth it to make it yourself. I can tell you right now that it is *always* worth it if you shop carefully.

Favors

You may be wondering why favors are given to guests at a wedding reception. This tradition goes back to the days when there was a lot of superstition about "good luck" and "bad luck." A bride and groom were considered "good luck," so guests used to tear off a bit of lace or ribbon from the bride's dress as a lucky souvenir, or they would snatch a flower from her bouquet. This evolved into the "bride's favors" being passed on to the guests in the form of keepsake remembrances; these favors are also given as a "thank you" to the guests for sharing the happiness of the day, and to pass on a little "good luck" or "good magic."

You don't need to overspend on your favors. There are dozens of clever ideas that are inexpensive to make yourself. Chapter three already offered several ideas. Here are a few more affordable ideas:

NETTED ALMONDS, POTPOURRI, SCENTED SOAPS OR BIRDSEED

Cut tulle netting into 9-inch circles, or order pre-cut packages (fifty to a package) of the netting. It is more expensive (about eighteen cents each) to use the pre-cuts, but may be worth your time. Wrap the netting around Jordan almonds, potpourri, soaps or birdseed; tie at the "neck" with personalized ribbon and a novelty decoration, such as a tiny white dove, candy cane, silk flower, etc. The personalized ribbon is imprinted with the names of the bride and groom, plus the wedding date. You can substitute narrow computer-generated cards that have the same information printed in a cursive or fancy font. Punch a hole in the card and tie it to the favor with a narrow satin acetate ribbon.

LACE POTPOURRI BAG

Purchase 5-inch-wide flat white lace or drawstring lace; cut into 8-inch lengths. Fold the lace in half crosswise, right sides together. Sew a narrow seam down the long side. Turn the lace right side out and top stitch about 1 inch up from the bottom.

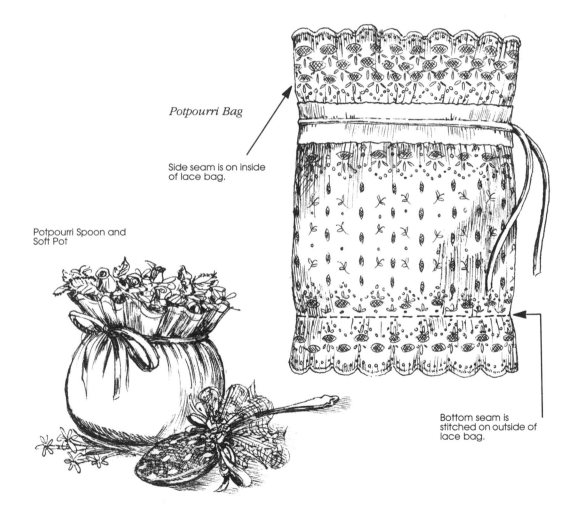

Potpourri Bag

Side seam is on inside of lace bag.

Potpourri Spoon and Soft Pot

Bottom seam is stitched on outside of lace bag.

Fill the bag with potpourri. If you're using plain lace, tie the bag at the neck with narrow satin ribbon or personalized ribbon; if you're using drawstring lace, draw the strings tight at the neck and then wrap with satin ribbon. *Optional:* If you have a Black and White wedding theme, use "see-through" lace and fill the bags with black licorice candy.

POTPOURRI SPOONS

Fill plastic or metal spoons with potpourri (look for antique teaspoons at garage sales or flea markets, or purchase single teaspoons from a factory outlet store). Wrap the end of the spoon with white bridal netting, gathering it up onto the spoon handle; tie with narrow ribbon and dried baby rosebuds. *Optional:* Fill each spoon with three chocolate kisses instead of potpourri. (See the illustration on page 99.)

SOFT SCULPTURE FLOWERPOTS

Plant herbs or bedding plants (petunias, impatiens, pansies, bachelor buttons, etc.) in a 3-inch clay flowerpot. Wrap the pot in heavy cellophane or foil (so the plants can be watered after the guests take them home). Then wrap each pot with polyester batting 1-inch thick (to give the soft sculpture wrap some puffiness). Finally, wrap the whole thing with calico or striped, plaid, flowered or polka-dotted cotton chintz fabric. Gather the fabric up around the rim of the pot and tie with colorful cording, ribbon or heavy yarn. What makes these pots so cute is their fat, puffy, padded look. (See the illustration on page 99.)

SEED PACKETS

Glue a personalized ribbon to a packet of flower seeds; add a calligraphied or computer-printed note that says:

> "As these seeds bloom, may the blossoms be reminders of our love for you.
> Thank you for sharing our special day."

If you enjoy writing, make up your own note, or compose a poem that can be attached.

DECORATED CANDLES

Here is a fun idea for an evening wedding: Wrap the base of a 12-inch candle in a 10-inch diameter circle of tulle netting. Tie the netting to the candle with narrow ribbon, adding a silk flower and 2-inch string of Pearls-by-the-Yard. For only about thirty cents a piece you can create not only a nice favor gift, but provide a dramatic exit for the bride and groom, as well. At the end of the reception give a candle to each guest; light the candles and have the guests stand on each side of the path that leads to the couple's getaway vehicle. The bride and groom walk down this lighted court as the guests say goodbye. It's a special ending to a special day.

TINY TREE SAPLINGS

Plant small conifer or other evergreen saplings in clay flowerpots that have been spray painted or left natural. Tie a ribbon around the base of each little tree, along with your personalized tag.

SHELL LEIS

If your theme is Polynesian, shell lei necklaces are the perfect favor. They are very inexpensive when purchased at oriental import shops (or is anyone vacationing in Hawaii between now and the wedding?). Add a computerized card (with the bride and groom's names and wedding date) tied to the lei with a ribbon. *Optional:* Add one fresh flower to each shell lei.

FOOD FAVORS

Wrap a piece of fruitcake or devil's food groom's cake in cellophane tied with a bow, or fill a tiny, square gift box (see chapter one) with homemade candy, cookies or speciality pastries. Tie the box with ribbon. Add a computer-generated card to each favor describing the contents and including the names of the bride and groom and the wedding date. Homemade fudge can also be cut into triangular pieces and wrapped in gold foil. *Optional:* Purchase boxes, already cut and ready to assemble (about eighteen cents each).

INSTANT PHOTOS FOR EACH GUEST

Have your amateur or professional photographer snap an instant photo of each guest or each couple as they enter the reception room. Attach a computer-printed card to each photo (with the names of the bride and groom and the wedding date) and hang the photos with narrow ribbons to a "photo tree" in the reception hall. Make an announcement inviting the guests to find their photos on the tree before they leave the reception. Let them know this is a gift from the bride.

CHRISTMAS ORNAMENT FAVORS

Wooden Rocking Horse

I've deliberately included this idea on the chance that the father-of-the-bride is feeling a little left out and needs something he can do to help. So, assuming he has an electric jigsaw, here's a terrific way for him to spend his time the next few weeks! First of all, enlarge the pattern shown below so the horse is about 7 inches long from "hoof" to "hoof." Use this pattern to cut wooden horses out of ½-inch-thick plywood or pine. Sand the horses until smooth, then spray paint them with flat enamel. Use a permanent black marker to dot the eyes; use your trusty glue gun to attach a straight candy cane to the bottom of the ornament. Tie a ribbon around the horse's neck, leaving a 4-inch loop to be used as a hanger. Write the names of the bride and groom on the horse's side, using a fineline glitter paint pen.

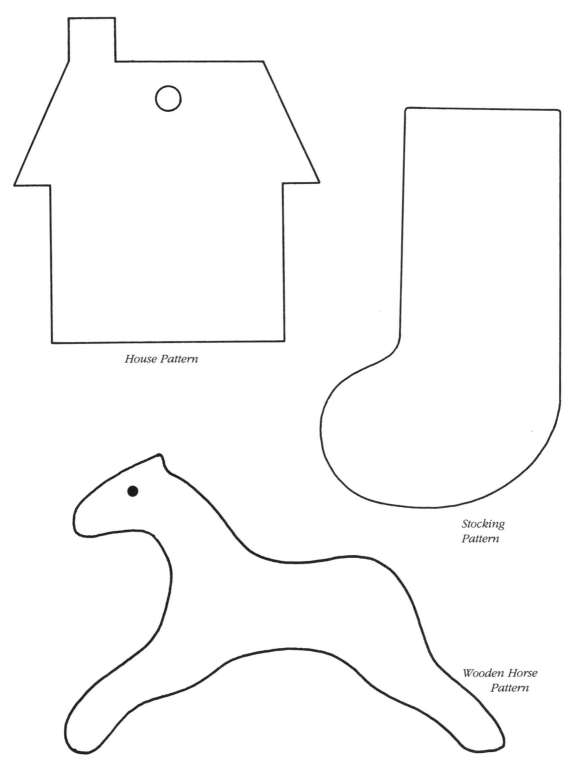

House Pattern

Stocking
Pattern

Wooden Horse
Pattern

Cookie House

Make a cookie house out of Christmas Ornament Dough, decorated with instant tube frosting or poster paint. Here is a foolproof recipe that will produce a firm "cookie" ornament that won't be as fragile as those made from ordinary cookie dough.

Christmas Ornament Dough

2 cups all-purpose flour

1 cup salt

2 tablespoons wallpaper paste

Water (as needed)

Combine the flour, salt and paste in a large bowl; add water gradually, mixing first with a fork, then with your hands, until the dough is no longer sticky. Turn the dough onto a work surface and knead for about 10 minutes until smooth. Roll out the dough on a lightly floured surface. Cut out a cardboard pattern, using the pattern shown on page 102. Place the pattern on the rolled dough and trace around it with a sharp knife. Use a thin spatula to transfer the "houses" onto a cookie sheet; skewer a hole in the top of the roof (to thread a narrow ribbon for hanging after the ornaments are completed); bake at 225 degrees until they are completely dry. Varnish the finished houses; let them dry. Decorate the houses with paint or frosting, writing the names of the bride and groom across the roof.

Note of caution: As you work, it is important that extra dough be covered with plastic wrap to keep it from drying out.

Bread Wreath Favor

Did you say your Grandma wants something to do? Ask her to help with these bread wreath favors. Purchase one 13¾-ounce box of hot roll mix for every fifteen bread wreath favors. Prepare the hot roll mix as directed on the label; let the dough rise in a warm place until doubled (about 40 minutes.) Turn the dough onto a lightly floured surface; let it rest for 15 minutes. Divide the dough into thirty equal pieces, then (with floured hands) roll each piece into a 12-inch-long rope (keep ropes covered with plastic wrap to prevent their drying out). Carefully twist two ropes of dough together, pinching ends together to form a circle. Place these wreaths on a lightly greased cookie sheet; cover and let rise until doubled (about 30 minutes). Bake in a pre-heated 375-degree oven for about 12 minutes. *Carefully* remove the bread from the cookie sheets with a thin spatula; cool the bread on wire racks. Decorate the wreaths by gluing red-hots in "flower clusters," or use tube frosting. Tie a bow around the top of the wreath (using ¾-inch red satin ribbon) that secures a computer-printed card that has the couple's names and wedding date. Leave a loop of ribbon for hanging.

Satin Stocking

Use the pattern below to cut stockings out of red satin fabric (or your wedding color, if you'd like). Fold the fabric in half; cut two pieces for each stocking. Place the two pieces with right sides together, then stitch around the stocking, very close to the edge, leaving the top open. Turn the stocking right side out and press with an iron. Stuff with cotton balls, then glue a strip of white cotton across the top of the stocking. Write the couple's names on the front of the stocking, using a liquid embroidery pen. Sew a 5-inch loop of narrow satin acetate ribbon to the top of the stocking as a hanger.

Seashell

If you already have a collection of seashells, or you live near the ocean and need a constructive reason to go beachcombing one of these Saturdays, here's a very inexpensive favor idea. Make ornaments out of seashells and ribbons. Any large shell will work, but the smoother the better. Wash the shells well. When dry, use a glittery fineline paint pen to write the couple's names across the front of each shell. Cut a 20-inch length of 1½-inch satin ribbon; loop it at the top of the length so that the ribbon crosses itself in the center of the back of the shell. Use your hot glue gun to attach the ribbon firmly to the shell. Press with your fingers until the glue is dry. Be sure to leave enough of a loop at the top to use as a hanger.

PERSONAL MESSAGE SCROLL

This idea has become very popular, not only because it is so inexpensive, but because it is a way for the bride and groom to thank their guests in a very personal way. The first step is for the bride and groom to compose a personal message; they can include poetry, a Bible verse or a saying, if they wish. Copy this message onto a "master" (have it calligraphied or it can be created on a computer using any cursive or fancy font). Take this master to a quick-print shop and copy it onto parchment paper approximately 8½″ × 14″ (nine messages per sheet). Cut out the individual messages with a paper cutter, roll each into a scroll, and tie with a satin acetate ribbon and two gold-colored rings. *Optional:* This is a time-consuming "extra," but worth it—tear the edge of the parchment paper so that when each scroll is rolled up, a ragged edge will show.

CHAMPAGNE GLASSES WITH JORDAN ALMONDS

Fill plastic champagne glasses with three almonds each; cover the entire glass with tulle netting, bringing it down to the stem of the glass. Tie the tulle with ribbon and a small silk flower. *Optional:* Fill the glasses with black licorice, wrap in cellophane and insert a straw. (This works well for a Black and White wedding theme.)

Rocking Horse Ornament
House, Shell, Stocking and Wreath Ornaments

MINIATURE BASKETS WITH JORDAN ALMONDS

Purchase tiny straw baskets (sold in plastic bags of ten baskets per bag). Follow the instructions given above for the champagne glasses, tying the tulle around the edge of the basket.

MINIATURE CACTUS PLANTS

Plant one cactus plant in a 2-inch clay flowerpot; tie a personalized ribbon around the neck of the pot.

Note: You probably noticed that I have not included rice in any of the favors; there's a reason for this. Rice is prohibited at most ceremony and reception sites, and using rice in favors is a bad idea because rice swells in the birds' stomachs and makes them sick. I recommend you throw birdseed instead.

All Those "Extra Little Things"

THE BRIDE'S THROWAWAY BOUQUET

Do I ever have an easy, but darling, idea for the bride's throwaway bouquet! Purchase a bush of silk roses (about twenty-four roses and buds, plus leaves). The stems of the flowers will already be bound into a "handle." Purchase 7 yards of 1½-inch ribbon lace, 1 yard of 4-inch white drawstring lace and 26-gauge craft wire. Gather the drawstring lace around the base of the bush; knot the string tightly and glue in place. Cut 10 inches of the ribbon lace and wrap around the bush stems (handle). Cut ten 16-inch lengths of the ribbon lace and fold each length into a double loop. Use a piece of wire to tighten and fasten each double loop deep into the bouquet; arrange the loops of ribbon lace evenly throughout the bouquet, then glue deep within the stems to hold them in position. Use the remainder of the ribbon lace to make a seven-loop full bow with streamers. Tie the bow to the front of the bouquet, using glue to hold it firmly in place. *Optional:* Add trailing silk ivy for a cascading bouquet.

SERVING ATTENDANT APRONS

Each apron requires ½ yard of white nylon lace or solid white satin acetate fabric (45 inches wide), 1 yard of 1½-inch white grosgrain ribbon, and 2½ yards of ruffled white lace (1 inch wide). Cut the fabric into 18-inch widths. When cutting the fabric, gently round the lower corners of the apron fabric. Gather the fabric along the 45-inch width, until the gathered edge is 20 inches wide. Center and pin the grosgrain ribbon to this gathered edge; stitch with a sewing machine. Top-stitch the ruffled lace onto the entire bottom and side edges of the apron fabric, folding the apron edges forward as you go (so there will be no raw edges showing). *Optional:* Add lace appliques, hanging pearls or silk rosettes as decoration. That's all there is to it!

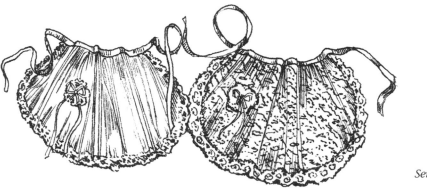

Serving Aprons

TOASTING GLASSES, CAKE KNIFE AND CAKE SERVER

You don't need to purchase expensive, engraved champagne glasses or a hand-painted, decorated cake knife and server. Instead use any champagne glasses you may already own, plus Grandma's antique sterling silver knife and server. Decorate all of them in the same way (they will be photographed together on the cake table). You can doll these items up as elegantly as you would like—anything from a simple white satin ribbon tied to the stems of the glasses and the handles of the knife and server, to added white silk stephanotis, tiny gold rings, 2-inch strings of Pearl-by-the-Yard, puffy tufts of tulle netting or fresh flower "lapel spray" arrangements.

GUEST BOOK AND PEN

Cover an ordinary "non-wedding" guest book with white satin, moire or taffeta fabric, using the directions already given for the Wedding Video Box in chapter one. Decorate a plain white plastic pen set by hot-gluing white feathers, narrow satin ribbon, tufts of tulle netting, or tiny white silk rosebuds on the pen's shaft.

A simple alternative to the guest book is a long piece of white parchment paper; roll it up tightly and then "let it unwind." Presto! You'll have a scroll for your guests to sign. After the wedding, frame the whole thing as a keepsake memento of the big day.

GIFT ENVELOPE OR FAVOR BASKET

Start with a rather "flat" basket with a tall handle; cover it and line it with flat white lace. Trim the edges and handle of the basket with ruffled lace. Add large lace bows on each side of the basket (where the handle attaches to the basket itself). *Optional:* Cover the basket with fabric that complements your theme, such as red velvet, pink polka dots, black and white taffeta stripes, etc.

6

The "Getaway" Vehicle

A limousine is long, sleek, sophisticated, impressive, mysterious and . . . boring! After you've attended as many weddings as I have, you get a little tired of the standard white limo. What we need is a better idea!

There are dozens of more interesting getaway vehicles out there, and we're going to talk about them in this chapter, along with innovative decorations as well.

Before deciding on a vehicle, there are several questions that need to be answered:

- Is this "getaway" just for the two of you, or for other members of the wedding party, as well?
- Are any of your attendants or groomsmen susceptible to motion sickness? Any afraid of heights?
- Is weather a factor? Can the vehicle be used in rain or snow?
- Will your gown survive the ride in the vehicle? Maybe you'll need to change clothes before your getaway.
- Have you actually tried out your plan? A dry run could save your big day. After all, what if your hoop-skirted wedding dress simply will not cram down into that rumble seat?
- Are there local ordinances prohibiting the use of certain vehicles? Do you need a special permit to parade through town? One simple call to the police station will ease your mind.

Now, let's consider a few alternatives to that boring white limousine; your choice depends on your spirit of adventure, your wedding's theme, and the degree of formality.

Vehicle Ideas

HORSE-DRAWN CARRIAGE

See the opening page of this chapter for a charming example. A horse-drawn carriage, with its fairy-tale style, is the ultimate in Cinderella elegance.

HORSE-DRAWN SLEIGH

If you live in an area where you can count on white, powdery snow for your winter wedding, this can be a Norman Rockwell getaway!

HELICOPTER

Here's where things get a little tricky—be sure it's legal for a helicopter to land at your site. Check with the local authorities.

CLASSIC CARS

If you're looking for a vehicle with its own distinctive personality, this idea is for you! Contact your local classic car club for names of their members who may be willing to loan or rent their vehicles. You may be able to escape in an old Rolls, T-Bird, Packard, or a pink Cadillac convertible.

Model A

ANTIQUE CARS

The "antiques" are older than the "classics" and have their own charm. How about a 1927 Hudson Super Six Four-Door Brougham, a 1939 Cadillac 60 Special, or any old Ford Model A with a rumble seat?

HOT AIR BALLOON

Take your vows on the ground, then float gently upward with a pop of the champagne cork and a toss of your bouquet. If this idea has appeal, however, you'll need a special permit and the weather will definitely become a factor, because hot air balloons won't sail in heavy winds.

BOAT

If you're getting married near a lake or river, you have several options: a sailboat, rowboat, speedboat, yacht or houseboat. Couples who marry up at Lake Tahoe not only leave via speedboat, but arrive at the ceremony site in a speedboat, as well. If the getaway is at dusk, there will be a romantic glow as you glide away over the water.

HORSES

If you and your groom are accomplished horseback riders, consider having a handsome pair of horses ready for the two of you to "ride off into the sunset."

CADILLAC OR LINCOLN TOWN CAR

Rather than pay $80 an hour, plus tips, to rent that long white limo, hunt around your family and friends for one of these impressive substitutes.

DECORATED JEEP

One of my readers sent me a photo of an old Jeep that had been converted into a fairy-tale float! They had wrapped it in white crepe paper (roll bar and all) and decorated it with big paper flowers, streamers and balloons. They "skirted" it with disposable, white plastic table skirting. No one ever knew there was an old rusty Jeep under there!

DECORATED PICKUP TRUCK

Use these same decorating ideas to convert any pickup truck into a "country-style convertible" with comfortable chairs set in the truck bed for you and your wedding party.

HAY WAGON

After the reception, prolong the celebration with an old-fashioned hayride. In one case, an entire wedding party clip-clopped up and down Main Street for a while, escorted the bride and groom to the airport, and then continued on their merry way as the couple flew off on their honeymoon. Add a little whimsy by renting a top hat for your driver.

SNOWMOBILE

Here is another cute idea for a winter wedding if you can depend on white, powdery snow at your site.

BICYCLE-BUILT-FOR-TWO

I've seen this done and is it ever a cute idea! Depending on your gown, you may want to change clothes before hopping onto this clever getaway vehicle.

MOPED OR MOTORCYCLE

If you're really into either of these modes of transportation, you're in luck because they provide terrific "photo opps." Be sure to decorate the helmets!

LITTLE YELLOW SCHOOL BUS

Two schoolteachers got married recently and their getaway vehicle was a small yellow school bus decorated with so many helium balloons the whole thing looked ready to "lift off"!

ANY CONVERTIBLE

It really doesn't matter what kind of car or what model year—as long as it's a convertible, it will work well. Keep in mind that everyone loves to see the bride and groom after the wedding! That's one of the big problems with those limos—the dark glass shuts everyone out. It may be fun on the inside, but it's pretty dull for the guests who are hoping to see the groom take his bride in his arms for a big "romance novel" kiss!

LITTLE RED TRACTOR

If you live in the country, or even if you don't, this novel idea is a photographic dream! There's nothing cuter than the bride and groom chugging away, dragging shoes, balloons, crepe paper streamers, and a couple of dozen cans.

COVERED WAGON

Depending on where you live, you may be able to rent a covered wagon, including horses and driver.

Pom-Poms,
Balloons
and Hearts

*Moped and
Bicycle-Built-for-Two*

MOTORIZED CABLE CAR

Many of you live in parts of the country that offer these nostalgic vehicles for rent, especially those of you who live in the San Francisco Bay Area. They will bring the cable car right to your site, load up the whole wedding party and more, then "trolley around town" as you ring the bell. Lots of fun!

Now that I've got you thinking "creative," "original," "exciting," "different" and "photogenic," let's talk about decorating these fun vehicles.

Decorating the Vehicle

"JUST MARRIED" CAR KIT AND "JUST MARRIED" CAR MARKERS

If the groom's "non-crafty" male friends are the ones who will be decorating the getaway vehicle, these kits are the perfect solutions. They are inexpensive, do-it-yourself, foolproof kits that provide pom-poms, streamers, "Just Married" signs, and harmless paint that will wash off safely with no damage to the car's finish. Purchase them at any wedding or party supply store.

OLD CANS AND SHOES

Traditionally, old cans and shoes have been tied to the bumpers of getaway vehicles. I don't know how the cans became popular, but I do know the origin of the shoes. In ancient times the Assyrians, Hebrews and Egyptians gave a sandal as a token of good faith when transferring property or making a deal. In fact, it became customary to throw a sandal onto a piece of land to show that the new owner was taking possession. Eventually, it became a British tradition for a father to give his new son-in-law one of the bride's shoes, signifying a transfer of authority. Today the bride's father ties old shoes to the bumper of the getaway car as a way of saying, "She's all yours now!"

BANNERS, SIGNS AND FLAGS

Make banners and flags (out of old sheets) or signs (out of poster board); write on them with poster paint or wide permanent felt-tip markers. The flags or banners can be attached to a tall antenna, if there is one; the poster board signs can be mounted on the back or sides of the vehicle. Try to come up with a saying that ties in with the bride's or groom's vocations or hobbies, such as:

"GOODBYE GOLF BUDDIES—HELLO NANCY!"

"HELLO MARRIAGE—GOODBYE BOOGIE BOARD!"

"THIS ONE'S SOLD!"
(If the bride or groom is in real estate.)

"THERE'S GONNA' BE A THREE-ALARM FIRE TONIGHT"
(If one is a firefighter.)

"GUESS WHO'S WEARING THE HANDCUFFS NOW!"
(If one is a peace officer.)

With a little imagination, you can think up dozens of ideas!

VOCATIONAL NOVELTIES

In the spirit of the idea just suggested, add trailing novelties denoting the couple's hobbies or occupations, such as old tennis rackets, golf clubs, swim fins, fishing poles, stethoscopes, old schoolbooks tied with belts, cross-country skis, a surf board or boogie board, real estate company "Sold" signs, handcuffs, a firefighter's hat, etc. *Be original!* As Winnie the Pooh has said, "THINK! THINK! THINK!"

PHOTO POSTER

Here's a great idea that's easy and fun! Take a photo of the couple and have it blown up into a large poster (reasonably priced at most drug store photo counters). Add the couple's names beneath their faces and attach the poster to the back of the vehicle, trailed by crepe paper ribbons, "Just Married" signs.

CREPE PAPER

Crepe paper is one good old tried-and-true way to decorate any vehicle. Stream it; wrap it around; tie it into bows; weave it in and out of spoked wheels, such as those on a buggy, bicycle-built-for-two, antique car, moped, carriage or hay wagon.

POM-POMS

Big, puffy pom-poms can be made or purchased through a catalog or at a wedding supply store. (See the illustration earlier in this chapter that shows the Chevy Bel Air convertible.)

RIBBONS, BALLOONS, TISSUE BELLS, TULLE NETTING

All of these decorations are easily affordable and accessible. The ribbon and tissue bells can be purchased at wedding or party supply stores; the tulle netting is available in fabric stores (about $1.19 per yard) and the balloons are sold everywhere. They don't necessarily have to be helium filled, by the way. The tulle netting can be draped from one end of the vehicle to the other with huge bows tied here and there. The tissue bells can be tied into the netting or topped with huge 10-yard satin acetate ribbon bows; the ribbons can be braided into the horses' tails.

THEME DECORATIONS

Decorate the vehicle in the spirit of the wedding's theme. If it's a Black and White theme, for example, use black and white streamers, posters, balloons or crepe paper. If the theme is holiday related, such as the Fourth of July, go crazy with red, white and blue everything, including plenty of American flags.

"GOD BLESS THE NEWLYWEDS"

You can purchase a triangular-shaped sign, outlined in red, with this saying. (It resembles a road sign.) Or you can make one yourself with poster board and poster paint or permanent felt markers.

OVERLAPPING HEARTS

Make two large overlapping hearts (enlarge the heart pattern in chapter one). Outline them in crepe paper flowers, pom-poms or garlands of greenery. Write the bride's name on one of the hearts and the groom's on the other. (See the illustration earlier in the chapter that shows these double hearts on the Bel Air convertible.)

GIANT DOVE

Enlarge the pattern shown opposite to cut a giant dove out of white poster board. Outline it in gold glitter or with any color felt-tip pen. Write the couple's name in the middle of the dove.

BOUQUET OF FLOWERS

Attach an actual bouquet of flowers to the front of the hood or grill of the car in such a way that the ribbons trail down and flutter in the breeze as the car drives away.

SINGLE FLOWERS AND GREENERY GARLANDS

Use huge, colorful crepe paper flowers (try the Mexican import shops), fresh or silk flowers, plus garlands of greenery.

I would love to have a photo of your getaway vehicle! If you have a spare, send a copy to me at my address given in the Epilogue of this book.

Dove Pattern

Flowers on a Grill

7

Groom's Gifts to His Ring Bearer and Groomsmen

The groom traditionally gives thank-you gifts to his groomsmen, ring bearer and any other junior male attendants. You couldn't very well have a wedding without all these men, and to show your appreciation, you will want to give each one an appropriate gift. These gifts are often given after the rehearsal dinner.

Gifts for the Men

Here are a few of the items usually given to the groomsmen:

Pen and pencil sets	Desk accessories
Key chain	Money clip
Cologne/toiletries	Travel kit
Wallet	Comb and brush set
Swiss army knife	Tie clasp or cuff links
Pewter tankard	Writing portfolio

These are all considered "safe" gifts, the type men have been receiving for years on their birthdays, Father's Days and Christmas mornings. I think most men already have enough of these generics to last a lifetime; I know my husband has a drawer full of cuff links, tie clasps and pins. What we need are some creative alternatives to these boring gifts, ideas that have more pizzazz! Why not give a gift so customized and special that it's bound to please?

Basket Gifts

In addition to the Beach Basket, Gardener's Basket, Picnic Basket and Coffee Basket already described in chapter one, here are three more personalized basket gifts for the guys.

"FOR THE GUY WHOSE CAR IS HIS SECOND HOME" BASKET

Some men practically worship their cars. If one or more of your groomsmen falls into this category, here's a "no-fail-guaranteed-to-please" gift! Fill a rugged, masculine-looking basket with an assortment of toys for your groomsman's "true love," his car. Browse around your local auto supply store and pick up a few of these practical basket fillers.

- Pressure gauge
- Amusing sunshade
- Can of air (for flat tires)
- Wide-bottomed coffee mug
- Change holder for tolls
- Small fold-up umbrella
- Map of the city
- Flashlight
- Windshield squeegee
- Car deodorizer
- Organizer for "over the hump"
- Chrome polish
- Car wax
- Windshield de-icer

Line the basket with tissue paper; tuck the items down into the paper, with the taller items (such as the sunshade) in the back of the basket. See the example on the opening page of this chapter.

SPORTS BASKET

Almost every man is into some kind of sport, even if it's only darts or Ping-Pong. Each basket will probably be different, of course, depending on the man's interests. Here are some possibilities for this fun basket:

- *Golf:* balls, tees, rule book, towel, instruction video, glove
- *Tennis:* balls, wrist- or head-band, racket-head cover, shirt, shorts
- *Skiing:* neck warmer, ski wax, goggles, gloves, ski mask
- *Cycling:* bike bag, hip pack, water bottle, gloves

- *Fishing*: lures, rod wires, flies, pliers, vest, net, rod case
- *Swimming*: trunks, earplugs, nose clips, goggles, waterproof wrist timer
- *Running*: Entry fee paid for a local race, wrist-bands with blinking lights, goggles, special sports socks that cushion feet
- *Softball or baseball*: balls, batting glove, baseball cap
- *"Indoor" sports*: chess sets, checkers and checkerboard, playing cards, table games

You can also add a little humor to the basket with first-aid supplies, a "crying towel" or a couple cans of his favorite beer. See the opening page of this chapter for an example of a sports basket with personality.

*Surprise Basket and
Gumball-Cookie Basket*

*Filled Wastebasket
and Fishing Creel*

"MONDAY NIGHT FOOTBALL" BASKET

Here's a basket for the sports enthusiast who would rather watch sports than play them. Depending on the date of the wedding, this basket can also be called the World Series Basket or the Super Bowl Basket. All the ingredients for this basket are selected for the "couch coach" or "replay commentator" in the group. Here are just a few novel fillers for this basket:

- A mug with his favorite team's logo
- Cheese and crackers
- Caramel corn or popcorn
- Chips and dips
- Smoked fish and meats
- Nuts
- A six-pack of his favorite drink
- A gift certificate for pizza delivery
- A referee's whistle
- A cigar
- A sports trivia book

A "Monday Night Football" basket is illustrated on the opening page of this chapter.

Other Gift Ideas

DECORATED BOTTLE OF WINE
Use the "shirt and tie" idea from chapter one (page 18), or simply tie a ribbon around the bottle's neck, along with a corkscrew. Use a "masculine" ribbon, such as a plaid or stripes.

FILLED WASTEBASKET
Purchase a wastebasket for his den or office, perhaps one with a sports-oriented motif, and fill it with any of these items:

- Fresh fruits
- Caramel corn
- Smoked sausage
- Cookies
- Chocolates
- Cheeses
- Pretzels
- Crackers
- Chips and dips

Or, fill the entire wastebasket with a huge plastic sack of popcorn or caramel corn you have popped and flavored yourself.

Tie the wastebasket with a wide plaid ribbon and you'll have a practical, appreciated gift—better than any ten key chains!

FILLED- FISHING CREEL

Use the same filler ideas given above, or add "cookie lollipops," a bottle of wine or champagne, beef sticks, sweet-hot mustard, honey-roasted peanuts, a plastic sack of the "Touchdown Party Mix," hot pepper cheese and crackers. This is an especially appropriate gift for the avid fisherman in your wedding party. Here is the easy recipe for cookie lollipops:

Cookie Lollipops

Make up chocolate chip cookie dough according to your favorite recipe. As you drop the dough onto your baking tray, add "lollipop sticks" (use candy apple sticks or popsicle sticks), inserting the sticks about half way into the dough. After the cookies are baked, *carefully* remove them from the tray, allow them to cool thoroughly, then wrap each "lollipop" in colored cellophane, tying at the neck with a ribbon.

GIFT CERTIFICATE

Don't underestimate the value of this gift! Use your computer to generate a gift certificate good for a home-cooked meal at your home (especially appreciated by the bachelors) or, for your married friends with children, how about a free night of babysitting.

FRAMED PRINT

Find an unframed print you know your friend would like, such as a reproduction of a Norman Rockwell painting or a famous golf hole or fishing stream. Select a masculine frame that will complement his den or office; mat the print yourself and be sure to use non-glare glass. By framing the print yourself, you will have an affordable gift that will rival those expensive framed prints seen in men's stores and gift shops.

Gifts for the Boys

Here are a few of the items usually given to ring bearers or junior attendants:

Two to Three Years Old

Ride-on trucks	Stuffed animals
Pop-up toys	Simple puzzles
Blocks or Legos	Books

Three to Six Years Old

Play telephones	Tool sets
Trucks	Stuffed animals
Electronic games	Fifty-piece puzzles

Six to Nine Years Old

Roller skates	One-hundred-piece puzzles
Table games	Craft/nature kits
Computer games	Books

A child should appreciate any gift you choose; however, if you want to give a gift that's special, here are some delightful alternatives.

Basket Gifts

"TOTE FULL OF FUN"

Fill a basket or tote with any of these fun-to-use fillers:

- Coloring books
- Paint-with-water books
- Sticker books
- Washable felt markers or crayons
- Glitter crayons
- Watercolors or poster paint
- Craft kits

Line the basket or tote with colored tissue paper, then tuck the gifts among the tissue. If you use a tote, you can personalize it by writing the boy's name on it with any permanent textile pen. Add a colorful bow.

GUMBALLS AND COOKIES

Wrap gumballs and cookies in colored cellophane; tie with ribbons. Fill the bottom of the basket with crushed tissue, then layer the gumballs and cookies until the basket is full.

SURPRISE BASKET

Fill an Easter-type basket with all kinds of little things you have picked up on sale, including:

- Little "hot" cars
- A whistle
- A harmonica
- Bath toys
- A ceramic bank
- Plastic soldiers, dinosaurs, and Batman, Superman or other figures

Your local version of the ninety-eight-cent store is a great place to shop for this surprise basket; they have "big bangs for a buck" that will thrill your little guy. Once the basket is full, wrap it in cellophane and tie it at the top with a large bow.

Other Gift Ideas

HUGE JAR OF PENNIES OR JELLY BEANS

Find or purchase a large clear plastic jar or container. Fill it with pennies or jelly beans—either way the boy will feel "rich." Tie a bright ribbon around the neck of the container.

TRUCK OR TOOL CHEST FULL OF CANDY

Purchase a large open truck or child's tool chest and fill it with candy (or cookies). Children like individually-wrapped Halloween-style candy or colorful piñata candy that can be purchased in big plastic sacks at many large supermarkets. Top the gift with a bright bow.

BOOKS AND TAPES

You know how expensive it is to purchase books with accompanying cassette tapes (where the story is read to the child as he flips the pages). Create your own affordable version by finding books on sale (appropriate to the boy's age level) and making your *own* accompanying story tape. Read the book out loud into a cassette recorder, indicating page turns with any soft noisemaker, such as a clicker, bell or pluck of a guitar string. Practice first until you have the story down pat, complete with different "voices" for the various characters. You can even add "commentary," such as, "Look, Jason, see the rabbit peeking out from behind the tree—I think he's watching the elephant walk by." You can give one book and story tape, or a set of several, perhaps by the same author. Wrap them in the Sunday newspaper comic pages and tie with a bright red ribbon. What an economical, yet personalized and appreciated gift!

MY OWN COOKIE JAR

Every child's dream is to own his very own cookie jar, *full* of cookies. Find a humorous cookie jar on sale (such as an animated cat or pudgy pig) and fill it with homemade chocolate chip cookies. Top with a ribbon, of course, and the boy will be prouder than the groom!

PERSONALIZED T-SHIRT

Purchase a T-shirt a size larger than the boy's regular size (to allow for the boy's growth and T-shirt shrinkage). Use any permanent textile pen or a liquid embroidery pen to write something clever across the front of the shirt, such as:

"I was a ring bearer in Bill and Anna's wedding, and all I got was this T-shirt" or "I was the ring bearer."

8

Bride's Gifts to Her Flower Girl and Bridesmaids

*t is proper etiquette for the bride to give thank-you gifts to her attendants, including her flower girl. These gifts are usually given during the bridesmaids' luncheon or after the rehearsal dinner.

Gifts for the Women

Here are a few gifts usually given to bridal attendants:

Pearl necklace	Gloves
Earrings or pin	Shoes
Bracelet	Heart-shaped locket
Handkerchief	Clock
Topiary	Compact
Picture frame	Scarf
Silver spoon	Jewelry box

It's even nicer, however, to personalize a gift especially for each woman, according to her hobbies or interests. Here are some creative ideas.

Basket Gifts

In addition to the dozens of basket gifts already described in previous chapters, here are three more, especially designed for women.

HOT CHOCOLATE BASKET

Fill a basket with colored excelsior, two mugs, packages of hot cocoa mix, mini-marshmallows and a small wooden spoon for stirring. Purchase the hot cocoa mix in bulk from a discount food supplier. Re-package the mix into your own plastic zipper bags wrapped in colored cellophane and tied at the "neck" with a ribbon. Add a wide gingham bow at the top or side of the basket.

BASKET OF HOMEMADE DESSERT BREADS

Bake your favorite nut, pumpkin or zucchini breads in miniature aluminum loaf pans. If you don't have your own favorite dessert bread recipes, you may use mine, given below. Wrap each individual loaf in clear plastic wrap and tie with dainty, feminine floral print ribbons. Place the bread in a basket lined with tissue paper. Make these dessert breads in advance and freeze them until the day they are placed in the baskets. See the dessert bread basket illustrated on the opening page of this chapter.

Pumpkin Bread

SIFT TOGETHER:
   3½ cups flour
   2 tsp. baking soda
   1 tsp. salt
   1 tsp. cinnamon
   1 tsp. nutmeg

ADD:
   3 cups sugar
   1 cup cooking oil
   ¾ cup water
   4 eggs
   2 cups canned pumpkin

   Stir together, then mix with an electric mixer for 3 minutes until smooth. Spray miniature loaf pans with cooking oil spray before adding batter. Bake at 350 degrees for 45 minutes. To see if baking is complete, press the top of a loaf and see if top springs back; if not, continue baking and check every 5 minutes. This recipe makes six to eight small loaves.

Zucchini Bread

BEAT TOGETHER:

6 eggs

4 cups sugar

4 tsp. vanilla

ADD:

2 tsp. baking soda

½ tsp. baking powder

2 tsp. salt

2 tsp. cinnamon

MIX IN:

4 cups cooked, mashed zucchini

1½ cups cooking oil

6 cups flour

MIX WELL, THEN STIR IN:

1 cup raisins

1 cup chopped nuts

Pour the mixture into miniature loaf pans sprayed with cooking oil. Bake at 350 degrees approximately 45 minutes. Then check to see if the top of a loaf springs back when lightly pressed with your fingers; if not, continue baking and check every 5 minutes. Makes about ten small loaves.

Banana Nut Bread

CREAM TOGETHER:

1 cup butter

2 cups white or brown sugar

ADD:

4 large well-beaten eggs

COMBINE THE FOLLOWING AND THEN ADD TO THE MIXTURE:

4 cups flour

1 tsp. salt

1 tsp. baking soda

FOLD INTO THE MIXTURE:

3 cups mashed bananas

1 cup chopped walnuts

Pour the mixture into miniature loaf pans coated with cooking oil spray. Let stand at room temperature for 20 minutes before baking, then bake at 350 degrees for 45 minutes to 1 hour. (They are done when the top springs back.) Makes eight to ten miniature loaves.

BASKET FILLED WITH BUTTON EARRINGS

Buttons are made from all kinds of materials—wood, glass, shells, leather, mother-of-pearl, plastic, metals, fabrics and ceramics. Depending on the differing personalities of your bridesmaids, you can custom-design earrings for each woman by glueing buttons onto earring backs. Purchase clip or pierced earring backs from your fabric or craft store. Glue the buttons onto the backs, creating inexpensive, yet original and attractive earrings. Because buttons are so affordable and easy to work with, you can make up a whole batch of earrings for each gal. Obviously, the "sew through" style button won't work for this venture; you will need to use buttons with a flat shank on the back. Go to your fabric store and check out their button drawers (where you can purchase individual buttons). There are also mail order sources for buttons, including handcrafted buttons, vintage buttons and imported European buttons, all listed in the Appendix. Once you have a supply of buttons and earring backs, use a trustworthy glue to attach the buttons to the earring backs. Tie each pair of earrings with colorful cellophane and ribbon. Arrange the earrings in a small, delicate basket (sprayed with gold glitter paint), lined with colored excelsior paper or Easter egg "grass." Wrap the entire basket with cellophane (like an Easter basket), tie at the neck with a satin acetate ribbon.

Other Gift Items

SET OF THREE SACHET PILLOWS

Make three satin sachet pillows; stack them on top of each other and tie them with a ribbon. Cut six pieces of heavy satin fabric, each 5″ × 5″ square. For each sachet pillow, place two pieces with right sides together; stitch close to the edges of the fabric, closing all sides, but leaving a 2-inch opening. Turn the piece right side out; press. Fill each pillow with soft cotton batting wrapped around crushed potpourri. Close the opening with invisible hand stitching. (A set of these pillows is illustrated on the opening page of this chapter.)

GIFT OF YOUR TALENTS

Make up a gift certificate for each bridesmaid. Depending on the woman, you can offer one night's free babysitting, an entire home-cooked meal brought to her door on the night of her choice, or a home-baked pie every month for a year, etc.

JEWELRY POUCH

Here is an easy, inexpensive gift idea for your bridesmaids—rich tapestry fabric jewelry pouches, each with ten soft velvet jewelry pockets.

For each pouch you will need one piece of heavy tapestry fabric, 10″ × 20″ and two pieces of black velvet, 10″ × 20″ each.

Stitch one piece of black velvet to the tapestry fabric, right sides together, leaving a 3-inch opening on one side. Turn right side out and press. Close the 3-inch opening by machine or hand stitching. Take the remaining piece of velvet and fold it lengthwise so that the right sides are together. Stitch the side and bottom seams, again leaving a 3-inch opening so the piece can be turned right side out. Once turned, press and close the opening by machine or hand stitching. Place this piece along the bottom of the larger piece; top-stitch the two pieces together at the dotted lines, as shown in the illustration below.

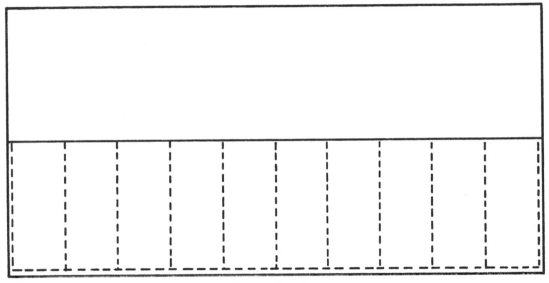

Jewelry Pouch

Now, you have ten jewelry pockets inside the pouch. Fold the top of the pouch down over the pockets, then roll the pouch, starting at one side. Tie with a length of black drapery cord.

DECORATED WATERING CAN

Find a simple or decorative watering can and spray paint it with silver or gold spray paint. Fill it with silk flowers and dried herbs. Let the shape of the pot dictate the arrangement; don't force a symmetrical design, but be sure the flowers and herbs look pretty from every side. By the way, some of the cutest watering cans are found in the children's toy department. (See the example illustrated on the opening page of this chapter.)

COUNTRY APPLE WREATH
Materials
    One 8-inch wire heart wreath (with hooks for opening and closing)
    One bottle lemon juice
    Ten unpeeled Rome apples
    Ribbon, ½ inch wide

Instructions

Cut the apples into ⅛-inch cross-section slices; coat them thoroughly with the lemon juice. Let the slices sit for 4 minutes. Place the slices on a broiler pan or wire screen and heat in a 200-degree oven for about 6 hours (until the apples are dried, yet pliable). Fold each slice in half, then in half again. Puncture each slice in the center, then thread onto the wire frame until the frame is full. Hook the ends together and add a ribbon at the top of the heart.

HOME-CRAFTED CHOKER

Cut a length of ribbon or braid, approximately 16 inches long; hand stitch Velcro to the ends of the ribbon or braid, to close the choker around the neck while wearing it. Use your hot glue gun to attach a decorative novelty to the front of the choker, such as a tiny framed cameo, an elegant or novelty button, a satin rosette or a silk flower.

Gifts for the Girls

Here are a few of the items usually given to flower girls or junior attendants:

Two to Three Years Old

Baby dolls	Barbie dolls
Pop-up toys	Simple puzzles
Blocks or Legos	Books

Three to Six Years Old

Fifty-piece puzzles	Barbie dolls
Books	Stuffed animals
A tea set	Polly Pocket sets

Six to Nine Years Old

Roller skates	One-hundred-piece puzzles
Table games	Craft/nature kits
Computer games	Books
Barbie/Ken dolls	

Many of the boys' gifts already suggested in chapter seven are also suitable for girls, such as the basket gifts, as well as the jar of pennies, book/cassette tape and cookie jar. Also, the T-shirt idea will work, only with different wording, of course: "I was a flower girl in Bob and

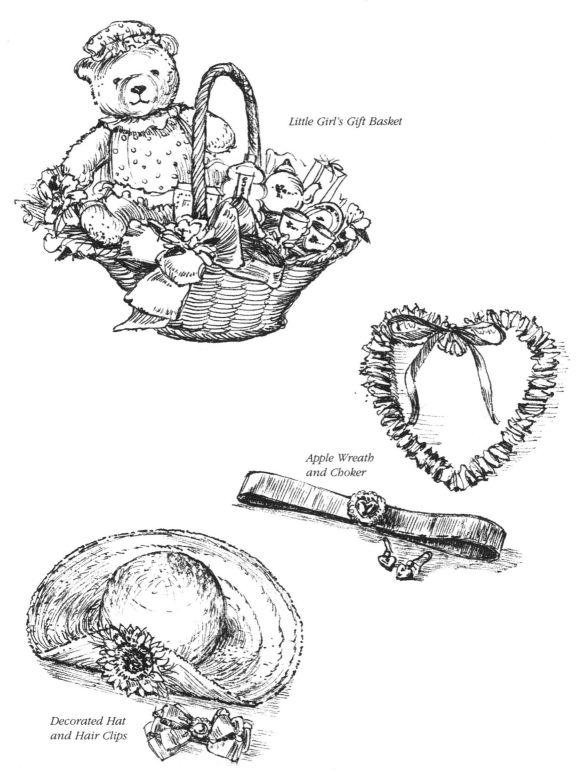

Little Girl's Gift Basket

Apple Wreath
and Choker

Decorated Hat
and Hair Clips

Anna's wedding, and all I got was this T-shirt" or "I was the flower girl in the wedding."
    Here are several more ideas, especially suitable for little girls.

Basket Gifts

THE BEAR THAT CAME TO TEA

Spray a basket with light pink paint; fill with pink excelsior. Add a stuffed bear, a complete child's plastic tea set and packages of tea. *Optional:* Add paper or cloth napkins and a tablecloth, tea biscuits or cookies.

CHILD'S BATH BASKET

This is a perfect gift for a two- or three-year-old girl. Fill a white basket with everything for her bathtub: rubber duck, bath toys, bubble bath, bubble blowing kit, decorative soaps and sponges. Nestle the items down into a basket lined with a couple of fancy feminine wash-cloths or hand towels. Wrap the basket with pink cellophane and tie it with a wide pink and white striped ribbon.

CHILD'S BEACH BASKET

Fill a basket with everything a little girl needs for fun at the beach: pail and shovel, wire strainer, beach ball, small Frisbie, child's beach towel, plastic water wings or tube, small plastic Jello molds, and other containers for building that perfect sand castle. *Optional:* Add a child's visor, sunscreen or sunglasses.

Other Gift Ideas

DECORATED HAT

Purchase a plain inexpensive straw or fabric hat and decorate it yourself by adding wide bands of silk or lace, raffia, big silk daisies or roses, along with a few silk leaves. You can turn a plain straw hat into a charmer by rolling up the front brim and securing it with a bright flower.

DECORATED HAIR CLIP

Use the same decorating ideas suggested for the flower girl in chapter four. (See page 78).

9

The Couple's Gifts to the Wedding Volunteers

t is thoughtful for the couple to give thank-you gifts to everyone who helps with the wedding, including:

- A friend or relative who housed a bridesmaid or groomsman for the night
- All unpaid musical performers
- Any friend or relative who contributes to the ceremony or reception by reading scripture, poetry, a tribute, etc.
- All children who help pass out programs, favors, rose petals or birdseed
- Guest book attendant
- Friends who help cut or serve the cake
- Friend in charge of your wedding gifts at the reception
- Friends who drove out-of-town guests to and from the airport, their lodging, the ceremony or the reception
- Volunteer babysitters
- Anyone else who has contributed in any way to your wedding

These gifts may be presented after the reception or as soon as the couple returns from their honeymoon. Here are some typical gifts for wedding volunteers:

- Framed photo of the bride and groom
- Framed wedding invitation
- Gift certificate

- Coffee mug set
- Perfume or cologne
- Tickets to a sporting event or concert
- Silver plate or bowl
- Crystal vase or paperweight
- Book

You also may use the gift ideas already given in chapters seven and eight for the bridesmaids and groomsmen, or you can make some of your decorations serve double-duty by giving them as gifts, such as the silk flower arrangements used at the rehearsal dinner, ceremony or reception, or any of the table centerpieces used at the rehearsal dinner or reception.

In addition to these ideas, here are eight more.

Basket Gifts

BAR-B-Q CHEF BASKET

This is a great gift for any man or woman who loves a cookout. Fill a large basket with all the goodies: charcoal, charcoal lighter fluid, potholder mittens, matches, barbecue tools, chef's hat and barbecue sauces. *Optional:* Follow the apron pattern in chapter one to make a customized apron; use any permanent textile pen or liquid embroidery pens to write a clever saying across the front of the apron, such as: "Don't Mess With the Cook" or "Tom— the Bar-B-Q Genius" or "Jason—Award Winning Chef."

PLANT IN A BASKET

What makes this gift special is the basket itself—it's not your ordinary woven basket, but one that is unique and eye-appealing with or without a plant. Find the nicest basket you can afford, then fill it with an inexpensive flowering plant from your discount nursery. Dress the basket with a fabric bow. See an example of this type of unique basket on the opening page of this chapter.

FRESH FRUIT BASKET

Everyone appreciates a practical gift like this, and you can shop for it right in your own supermarket. Find a deep, round basket with a handle and fill it with the most beautiful fresh fruits you can find, including pineapple, apples, pears, peaches and grapes. (Don't include bananas because they spoil too quickly.) Nestle the fruits in excelsior or Easter basket grass, building the basket from back to front with the taller fruits in the back and the smaller toward the front. *Optional:* Add silk flowers and greenery among the fruits. Wrap the entire basket with cellophane and tie the top with a gingham fabric bow.

Bundt Cake and Fruit Basket

Other Gift Ideas

DECORATED BUNDT CAKE

A simple Bundt cake can become a work of art by simply placing the cake on an expensive looking plate, tucking a silk nosegay into the center hole of the cake, then wrapping it, plate and all, with cellophane and tying with a bow. You might find a single china dinner plate for sale at a garage sale or flea market, or purchase the sturdiest, prettiest paper plates you can find. If you happen to find an especially fine china dinner plate at a garage sale, it will make the gift seem extra special. *Optional:* Use a sifter to shake confectioner's sugar onto the top of the cake before inserting the nosegay. By the way, this cake can be baked a month ahead of time and frozen until the wedding.

GIFT JAR OF HOMEMADE BISCOTTI

You know how certain foods become fads from time to time; well, this year it's biscotti! Biscotti is inexpensive and easy to make yourself; the trick is to find a unique clear glass container, such as an apothecary jar, old Mason jar, cookie jar or any attractive glass storage container. Try the oriental import shops and factory outlet kitchen stores for distinctive glassware. These stores also sell inexpensive, but attractive, cork-top storage containers that will work as well. Cut a circle of checked or flowered gingham fabric and wrap it over the lid of the container, securing with a piece of raffia or ribbon. Add a little card that says, "Homemade by . . . " so the gift has that personal touch. *Optional:* Purchase store-bought biscotti from your supermarket or bakery and use them to fill your own containers. See an example of a decorated jar full of biscotti illustrated on the opening page of this chapter.

If you don't happen to have a recipe for biscotti, I will share mine with you:

Biscotti

⅓ cup margarine or butter
2 cups all-purpose flour
⅔ cup sugar

2 eggs

2 tsp. baking powder

1 tsp. vanilla

1½ cups almonds, finely chopped

¼ tsp. cinnamon

1 egg yolk (optional)

1 tablespoon milk (optional)

Beat margarine or butter with an electric mixer on medium speed for 30 seconds (or until softened). Add 1 cup of the flour, the sugar, the 2 eggs, baking powder and vanilla; beat until combined. Stir in the remaining flour and nuts, then divide the dough in half. Shape each half into a log about 9″ × 2″. Place the logs about 4 inches apart on a lightly greased cookie sheet. (For shine, stir together the egg yolk and milk and brush onto the logs.) Bake at 375 degrees for about 25 minutes; cool on the cookie sheet for 1 hour. Cut each log diagonally into ½-inch-thick slices. Lay the slices on an *ungreased* cookie sheet and bake again, this time at 325 degrees for 8 minutes, then turn the slices and bake another 8 or 10 minutes until dry and crisp. Cool on a wire rack. Makes about three dozen pieces of biscotti.

Biscotti is great for gift-giving because you can bake it two or three weeks ahead of time; just be sure the container is kept tightly sealed.

GRAPEVINE WREATH

Decorate a 12-inch grapevine wreath with silk flowers, silk leaves, a small bluebird and a 1-yard bow. Set the flowers, bird and bow at the bottom of the wreath; use the leaves to fill in the top and sides. With heavy-gauge florist wire, form a hanger at the upper back of the wreath.

Wreath With Bird

JARS OF "HOME-COOKIN'"

If you love to can fruits or vegetables, or cook up your own special jams, jellies, mustards or sauces, give one jar of your home-cookin' to each helper. The trick is to decorate the jar itself in such a way that it becomes something out of the ordinary. Use a circle of gingham to cover and wrap the top, or tie with raffia or ribbon, or decorate with silk flowers and greenery. And, of course, always add your "Homemade by . . ." card, which is what makes this simple gift very meaningful and personal for each recipient. (See a couple of examples on the opening page of this chapter.)

CRAZY QUILT

If you really want to impress friends or relatives with what will seem to them an *incredible* gift, make crazy quilts. This is one of those "sneaky" gifts that seems to be difficult and time-consuming to make, but, in actuality, is an "easy-no-way-to-fail-even-a-beginner-can-make-one" kind of a project. Take a look at the crazy quilt draped over the chair on the opening page of this chapter. Isn't it great? Here are the easy directions:

Materials

- Remnants of any fabrics that are "fuzzy" or "nappy," such as velvet, terry cloth, corduroy, velour or fake fur
- One old queen size flat sheet (any color)
- One new queen size flat sheet (in a dark or bright color that complements the colors in your remnant fabrics)
- Yarn the same color as the new sheet
- One large-eyed needle (for use with the yarn)

Instructions

Cut forty-eight squares (12½ inches each) from the old sheet. (These will be used as backing for the individual squares of crazy-quilted fabric pieces.) Cut random pieces out of your remnant fabrics, using the pattern pieces numbered 1, 2, 3 and 4 shown on pages 144 and 145. Machine stitch these pieces together in any "crazy" pattern you wish, until you have "almost-squares" that are a little larger than 12½ inches each.

Place each of these squares of pieced fabric on top of one of the forty-eight squares cut from the old sheet, trimming the "crazy" piece to fit exactly on top of the 12½-inch square cut from the old sheet. Sew the pieced fabric square and the old sheet square together at the edges.

Continue this process until you have completed forty-eight squares. Sew these squares together into eight rows of six squares each. Sew the eight row together. You have now completed the front of your crazy quilt. Place the front of your quilt flat (right side showing) against the new queen size sheet; pin the two pieces together at the outside edges. Trim the sheet leaving 3 inches extending around all four sides of the quilt. Use this extra fabric to fold up onto the front of the quilt to form binding. Pin the fabric in place and then top-stitch, using your sewing machine, sewing through from front to back of the quilt. (By the way, no

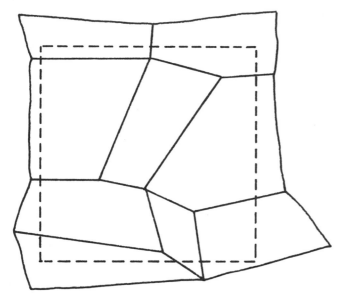

Quilt Square

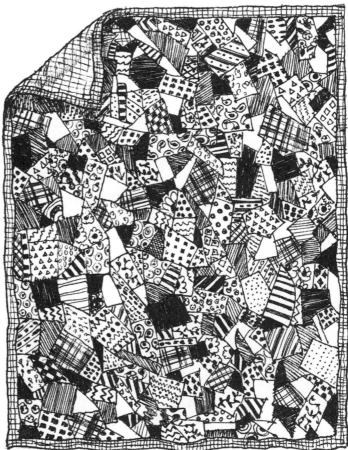

Crazy Quilt

batting is required because of the triple thickness: two layers of sheeting and the top layer of rather heavy, nappy fabrics.)

For the final step: Thread the large-eyed needle with the yarn and sew through all layers of the quilt every 12 inches. Take a single stitch through the layers. Cut the yarn about 6 inches away from the quilt and tie the yarn in a double knot. Trim the ends of the knot about 2 inches away from the quilt. *Optional:* Use the yarn to make decorative, "exaggerated" stitches, connecting the various crazy quilt pieces on the front of the quilt (the pieces have actually been machine-stitched together and these giant stitches are just for "show"). (See the quilt illustrated on the opening page of this chapter.) When the quilt is finished, this is what it should look like when it's laid out flat:

As you can see, this is an easy, quick way to make a quilt; it should only take a few hours from start to finish, once you have all your materials together. Helpful hint: if you want your quilt to take even less time, enlarge and use the pattern pieces shown on pages 144 and 145.

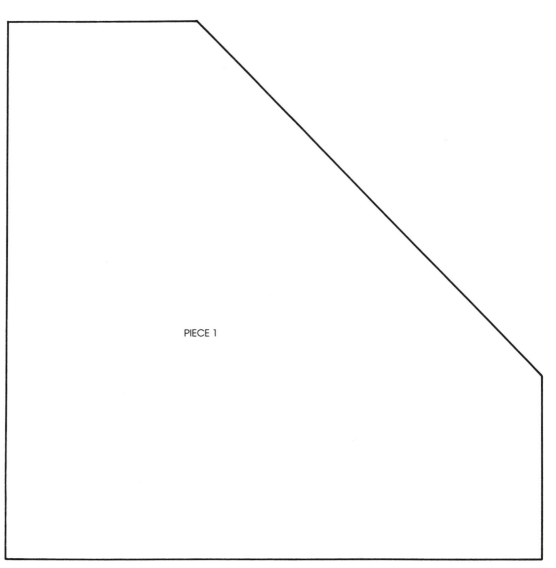

PIECE 1

Quilt Pattern No. 1

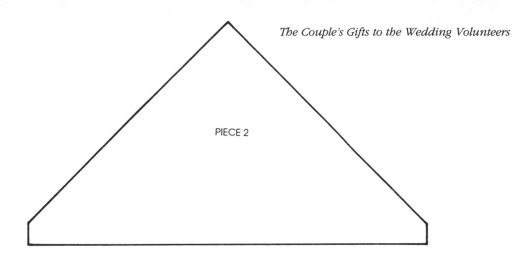

PIECE 2

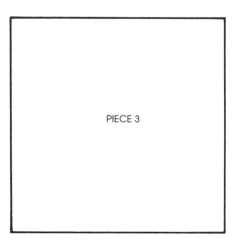

PIECE 3

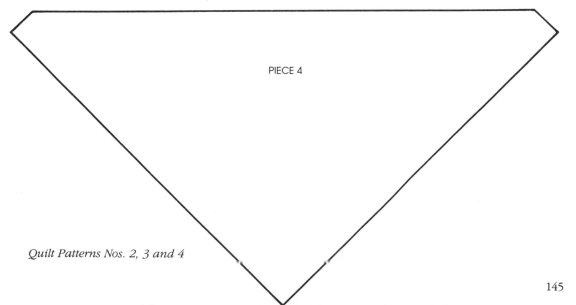

PIECE 4

Quilt Patterns Nos. 2, 3 and 4

10

The Couple's Gifts To Their Parents

inally, we come to the most important gifts of all—the couple's gifts to their parents. These are usually of a permanent nature, the type of gifts that are treasured forever as keepsakes or mementos of the wedding. Give these gifts a lot of thought, and be sure to accompany them with a loving thank-you note.

These are a few of the traditional gifts given to the parents:

- A silk or live plant
- Framed wedding invitation
- Fruit, cheese or wine basket
- Framed poem or thank-you note
- A singing telegram the day after the wedding

Here are a few gift ideas already presented in this book that work well for the parents:

SECOND HONEYMOON PICNIC BASKET
Use the Honeymoon Picnic Basket idea from chapter one; after all the work your parents have done for your wedding, encourage them to take off on a second honeymoon, even if only for a romantic picnic with their very own honeymoon basket.

WEDDING MEMORABILIA BOX
Also from chapter one, steal this idea for the parents. Fill a box with keepsakes from your wedding: Dad's pressed boutonniere, Mom's preserved corsage, the invitation and ceremony program, and snips of ribbon and other items from the ceremony and reception decor.

DRESSED-UP CHAMPAGNE BOTTLE

After what your parents have been through to get you married, they deserve to celebrate privately with their very own bottle of champagne. Add a touching "thank-you" tied to the neck of the bottle, along with a couple of champagne glasses and a quality corkscrew. You can find directions for "dressing" the bottle in chapter one.

DECORATED VIDEOTAPE BOX

Use the directions in chapter one to create a special wedding videotape storage box.

WEDDING PHOTO ALBUM

Use the directions in chapter two to create a satin and lace covered album for your parents.
Here are seven more gift ideas especially for the parents:

THANK-YOU BOOK

Purchase a "blank book" from your local book store or stationery store; fill it with remembrances of all the loving, precious things your parents have done for you, all the memorable family times that mean so much to you now. You can even add snapshots of you and your parents when you were younger, with comments such as, "Thanks for always being there for me, even when I insisted on buying this old pile-of-junk pickup," or "Thanks for always being there to dry my tears."

WEDDING MEMORY TOPIARY

Use the directions in chapter two to build a special wedding memory topiary for your parents, adding dried flowers and pieces of ribbon from the bride's bouquet along with any decorative accessories used in the wedding or reception. Depending on your wedding theme, you may also want to add small love doves or double rings, along with a couple of wedding favors. You can even add tufts of fabric from the bridesmaids' or mothers' dresses. This will become a family keepsake for all the years to come.

GIFT CERTIFICATE

Design an elegant gift certificate "good for one special evening in honor of our parents," including dinner at a fine restaurant and sharing of wedding and honeymoon photos and memories.

EMBROIDERED OVAL

If you enjoy embroidering, design an oval-shaped piece of handwork with two hearts entwined, the names of the bride and groom, plus the wedding date. Add any delicate borders you wish, such as small rosebuds mixed with ivy. Frame this precious keepsake in a white ceramic or brass frame.

Wedding Memory Topiary

Framed "Thank-You"

SILK REPLICA OF THE BRIDAL BOUQUET

This is a popular choice lately: Create a silk replica of the bride's bouquet, duplicating all the fresh flowers and greens with silks.

DOUBLE-FRAMED TRIBUTE

Purchase a double frame with a center hinge. On one side mat a photo of the bride and groom or the parents; on the other side mat a calligraphied or computer-printed "Dear Mom and Dad" tribute or thank-you letter.

WEDDING TREE

Purchase a live, potted evergreen tree and present it to your parents to be planted in their yard as a remembrance of your wedding day. It will always be known as "Bob and Anna's tree." The tree will be *ever* green, a symbol of your everlasting love and appreciation for your parents. The tree will grow each year, a symbol of the bride's and groom's ever-growing love for each other. Attach a card or thank-you letter that expresses these sentiments.

Epilogue

WARNING: The successful completion of any project within the pages of this book *may* lead to an addicting disorder known as: *do-it-yourself-itis*! You may never be able to walk into a store and pay retail again!

*O*nce you've experienced the "joy of creation," you may even become one of those *serious* crafters; you know, the type who actually make quilts the *hard* way. It is so satisfying to make something with your own hands, to give personalized gifts that really *mean* something, and to save money at the same time. By giving of yourself, you not only create something unique and special, but you give away your love as well, and your love is worth more than all the gold in town.

I know you have wonderfully creative ideas of your own, and I would love to hear about them. Please write me in care of my publisher:

Diane Warner
c/o Betterway Books
4700 East Galbraith Road
Cincinnati, Ohio 45236

Appendix

The Ceremony

Blayney, Molly. *Wedded Bliss: A Victorian Bride's Handbook*, New York, London, Paris: Abbeville Press, 1992.

Bride's Magazine. *Bride's Little Book of Customs and Keepsakes*, New York: Clarkson N. Potter, 1994.

——*Bride's New Ways to Wed*, New York: Perigee/Putnam, 1990.

——*Bride's Shortcuts and Strategies for a Beautiful Wedding*, New York: Perigee/Putnam, 1986.

Brown, Gail and Karen Dillon. *Sew A Beautiful Wedding*, Portland, Oregon: Palmer/Pletsch Associates, 1980.

Church, Beverly. *Weddings Southern Style*, New York: Abbeville Press, 1993.

Clark, Beverly. *Planning A Wedding to Remember*, Carpinteria, California: Wilshire Publications, 1989.

Clark, Leta. *Affordable Weddings*, New York: Simon and Schuster, 1988.

Dlugosch, Sharon. *Wedding Plans*, New Brighton, Minnesota: Brighton Publications, 1989.

Fabian, Carole Ann and Linda Franklin. *A Wedding Notebook for the Bride*, South Salem, New York: The Country Diary Company, 1989.

Kirkham, Jenni. *The Wedding Craftbook*, Australia: Kanagroo Press, 1994.

Packham, Jo. *Wedding Gowns and Other Bridal Apparel*, New York: Sterling Publishing, 1994.

Tatsui-D'Arcy, Susan. *The Working Woman's Wedding Planner*, Englewood Cliffs, New Jersey: Prentice Hall, 1991.

Tober, Barbara. *The Bride—A Celebration*, New York: Longmeadow Press, 1992.

Warner, Diane. *How to Have a Big Wedding on a Small Budget*, Cincinnati: Writer's Digest Books, 1992.

Warner, Diane. *Big Wedding on a Small Budget Planner and Organizer*, Cincinnati: Writer's Digest Books, 1992.

Crafts Supplies

Aleene's
    P.O. Box 68, Temple City, AZ 91780 (craft glues)

Boyd, Margaret A. *The Crafts Supply Sourcebook* (*Shop-By-Mail Guide*), Cincinnati: Betterway Books, 1994.

Britex
    146 Geary Blvd., San Francisco, CA 94108 (buttons, notions, trims)

Button Shop
    P.O. Box 1065, Oak Park, IL 60304

Discount Crafts Supplies Catalog
    4320 31st St. N., St. Petersburg, FL 33714

Floracraft
    1 Longfellow Pl., Ludington, MI 49431 (crafting with Styrofoam)

Thomson, George. *The Calligraphy Work Book*, New York: Sterling Publishing, 1985.

Tulip Productions
    180 Elm St., Waltham, MA 02154 (fabric paints)

Etiquette

Dunnan, Nancy and Nancy Tuckerman. *The Amy Vanderbilt Complete Book of Etiquette*, New York: Doubleday, 1994.

Post, Elizabeth L. *Emily Post's Complete Book of Wedding Etiquette*, New York: HarperCollins, 1991.

Flowers

Cazenovia Abroad
    67 Albany St., Cazenovia, NY 13035 (tussie mussie holders)
Bride's Magazine. *Bride's Little Book of Bouquets and Flowers*, New York: Clarkson N. Potter, 1993.
McBride-Mellinger, Maria. *Bridal Flowers*, New York: Little, Brown and Company, Inc., 1992.
Packer, Jane and Elizabeth Wilhide. *Flowers for All Seasons*, New York: Fawcett Columbine, 1989.
Reppert, Bertha. *Herbs for Weddings and Other Celebrations*, Pownal, Vermont: Storey Communications, Inc., 1993.
Vanessa-Ann. *Flowers for a Friend*, New York: Meredith Press, 1993.

Pre-Wedding Parties

Clark, Beverly. *Showers*, Carpinteria, California: Wilshire Publications, 1989.
Dlugosch, Sharon, and Florence Nelson. *Bridal Showers: Fifty Great Ideas for a Perfect Shower*, New York: Perigee/Putnam, 1987.
Sowden, Cynthia. *Wedding Occasions*. New Brighton, Minnesota: Brighton Publications, 1994.
Stewart, Martha and Elizabeth Hawes. *Entertaining*, New York: Clarkson N. Potter, 1982.
Tapper, Hans. *Great Napkin Folding and Table Setting*, New York: Sterling Publishing, 1990.

The Reception

Bride's Magazine, *Bride's Little Book of Cakes and Toasts*, New York: Clarkson Potter, 1993.
Burbridge, Cile. *Cake Decorating for Any Occasion*, Radnor, Pennsylvania: Chilton Book Co., 1978.
Greger, S. *A Guide to Decorating With Balloons*, Cedar, Minnesota: Greger Enterprises.
Macgregor, Elaine. *Wedding Cakes*, London: Merehurst Limited, 1988.

Rentals

American Rental Association
    1900 19th St., Moline, IL 61265 (ask for their "Party Rental Guide")

Index